Cambridge Elements ≡

Elements in the Philosophy of Immanuel Kant
edited by
Desmond Hogan
Princeton University
Howard Williams
University of Cardiff
Allen Wood
Indiana University

KANT AND THE FRENCH REVOLUTION

Reidar Maliks
University of Oslo

CAMBRIDGE
UNIVERSITY PRESS

CAMBRIDGE
UNIVERSITY PRESS

University Printing House, Cambridge CB2 8BS, United Kingdom

One Liberty Plaza, 20th Floor, New York, NY 10006, USA

477 Williamstown Road, Port Melbourne, VIC 3207, Australia

314–321, 3rd Floor, Plot 3, Splendor Forum, Jasola District Centre,
New Delhi – 110025, India

103 Penang Road, #05–06/07, Visioncrest Commercial, Singapore 238467

Cambridge University Press is part of the University of Cambridge.

It furthers the University's mission by disseminating knowledge in the pursuit of
education, learning, and research at the highest international levels of excellence.

www.cambridge.org
Information on this title: www.cambridge.org/9781108438735
DOI: 10.1017/9781108529723

First published 2022

A catalogue record for this publication is available from the British Library.

ISBN 978-1-108-43873-5 Paperback
ISSN 2397-9461 (online)
ISSN 2514-3824 (print)

Kant and the French Revolution

Elements in the Philosophy of Immanuel Kant

DOI: 10.1017/9781108529723
First published online: February 2022

Reidar Maliks
University of Oslo

Author for correspondence: Reidar Maliks, reidar.maliks@ifikk.uio.no

Abstract: To Kant, the French Revolution's central events were the transfer of sovereignty to the people in 1789 and the trial and execution of the monarch in the period 1792–3. Through a contextual study, this Element argues that while both events manifested the principle of popular sovereignty, the first did so in lawful ways, whereas the latter was a perversion of the principle. Kant was convinced that historical examples can help us understand political philosophy, and this Element seeks to show this in practice.

Keywords: Kant, French Revolution, popular sovereignty, revolution, reform

ISBNs: 9781108438735 (PB), 9781108529723 (OC)
ISSNs: 2397-9461 (online), 2514-3824 (print)

Contents

1 Introduction and Historical Context

Most scholars believe that Kant strongly supported the French Revolution and its ideals of *liberté, égalité, fraternité*, even though he could not justify a right of revolution. Kant admired the enthusiasm of the spectators who sympathised with the French nation's efforts to provide itself with a republican constitution, saying, in *Conflict of the Faculties*, 'such a phenomenon in human history will not be forgotten, because it has revealed a tendency and faculty in human nature for improvement' (CF 7: 88). Other sources supporting scholars' claims that Kant was a sympathiser include contemporary accounts citing his Königsberg reputation as a 'Jacobin', anecdotal information relating his single-minded interest in the topic, and his staunch dinner party defences of the event. When the republic was declared, he apparently said, 'Now let your servant go in peace to his grave, for I have seen the glory of the world'.[1]

Yet this reading of his sympathies must be inaccurate, for the simple reason that the French Revolution was a complex historical event, some parts of which Kant wholeheartedly endorsed, while condemning others in the strongest possible terms. This Element looks beyond the received version and argues for a nuanced view. It aims to present a more contextually sensitive analysis of popular sovereignty, an underlying principle of both the revolution and Kant's political philosophy. Historians often distinguish between *two* revolutions in France: the liberal one in 1789, then the radical one in 1792.[2] This Element explores Kant's detailed analysis of the philosophical justifications of each. He saw the first as an instance of a legitimate reform leading to the people taking power, and the latter as one of lawless popular rebellion.

The first revolution began in the spring of 1789, when King Louis XVI, an absolute monarch, summoned the Estates General, the ancient assembly of nobility, clergy, and commoners, to deliberate in Versailles about the nation's problems. In June, the commoners, claiming to speak for the nation as a whole, rejected the king's sovereignty and demanded recognition as a National Assembly. The king's capitulation precipitated the institution of a constitutional monarchy, which was philosophically justified in terms of popular sovereignty. Popular participation in the constitutional transition from autocracy to constitutional rule was the key issue for Kant. He considered the people's will an ideal standard for public justice, and the public sphere as an essential space for the expression of political views. But the people's will and actions could only be legally binding if they were established

[1] Manfred Kuehn, *Kant: A Biography* (New York: Cambridge University Press, 2001), p. 342.

[2] Francois Furet, *Revolutionary France: 1770–1880*, translated by Antonia Nevill (Oxford: Blackwell Publishing, 1988), p. 109; Albert Soboul, *A Short History of the French Revolution 1789–1799* (Berkeley: University of California Press, 1977), pp. 38 and 84.

within a constitutional framework. Without proper institutions, there are no stand-ards to distinguish between the views of a faction and the will of the whole. This raises the issue of the people's role in changing the very constitutional structure that authorises its collective voice. What authorised the commoners to claim that right? And did they act legitimately on behalf of 'the people', or were they just one political class with no right to speak on behalf of the whole? Kant believed the answer lay in what he claimed was the king's abdication, and the people's right to act through a representative assembly.

The second revolution began in August 1792, when radical factions accusing Louis XVI of plotting counter-revolution stormed the Tuileries Palace, imprisoned the king, abolished the National Assembly, proclaimed the republic, and judged and executed the king, despite his constitutional inviolability. For Kant, these events raised the issue of a popular right of resistance, and the associated right to act as judge and jury over the sovereign. It also raised the issue of whether regicide can ever be justified by appealing to a right of necessity, and of the instrumental use of law for the sake of covering up what are actually crimes. Finally, it raised questions about whether a former sover-eign who has been unjustly deposed may seek to regain power.

This Element argues that Kant's response to these questions is grounded in the requirement that popular sovereignty be expressed through representation within a constitutional system. Kant sympathises with the commoners' deputies in 1789 because, unlike the rabble-rousers on the streets of Paris in 1792, they did not use force against an existing regime. The two events illustrate the legitimate and illegitimate roles 'the people' can play in political transformations. In the first case, the people acted indirectly, through their representatives, who deliberated in a public forum that had a legal foundation; in the second, the people, led by agitators, took the law into their own hands, stormed the seat of the executive power (the royal palace), and then instrumentalised law for political ends.

Although there is extensive scholarly literature on Kant's views of resistance and revolution in general, his juridical discussion of the example of the revolu-tion in France has attracted less attention. Kant's views of the French Revolution are typically deduced from his view of the revolution as an historical event, which he discusses in *Conflict of the Faculties*, but that discussion is not about the juridical principles that were at stake (I will return to that at the end).[3]

---

[3] Christian Ferrié, for example, has recently argued that Kant legitimated the use of revolutionary violence because he thought history naturally develops through violent revolutions, excused the regicides by their fear of counter-revolution, and was given hope for mankind's moral improve-ment by the spectators' enthusiasm for the struggle for freedom. Such historical explanations do not, however, amount to a justification of the use of force to overthrow a government. See Ferrié, 'Le réformisme en révolution', in *La Pensée* 386, no. 2 (2016): 64–77. Domenico Losurdo made similar claims in *Immanuel Kant: Freiheit, Recht und Revolution* (Köln: Pahl-Rugenstein, 1987).

His juridical views are difficult to understand because they analyse the significance of historical and legal facts in light of both his own legal and political principles, and those of the actors themselves. Making sense of them may sound like an arcane enterprise, but it is worth our time. Kant intended his analysis of the revolution to illuminate the principles developed in *The Metaphysical First Principles of the Doctrine of Right*, the first part of the *Metaphysics of Morals*, from 1797. The treatise, which today would be called jurisprudence or legal philosophy, is, as the name indicates, a system founded on reason. Kant applies these a priori principles to the empirical cases of the Estates General and the trial and execution of the monarch (these reflections are indented and in footnotes so that his readers could tell the difference). Assuming the role of judge, he applies standards to specific circumstances, formulating tests to explicate the significance of abstract legal principles. Kant thought his examples from France could 'throw light on the principles of political rights' (MM 6: 321). We can hope to learn how Kant himself understood his metaphysical principles by observing how he sought to parse reality accordingly. We can also hope to gain unexpected perspectives on the past.

Karl Marx famously stated in 1842 that '*Kant's philosophy* is rightly to be regarded as *the German theory* of the French Revolution'.[4] Several authors have followed Marx in claiming that Kant's turn to politics in the 1790s was a direct response to the revolution.[5] This might seem intuitive, since all his published attempts to justify principles of right came in the wake of the revolution. Yet, this cannot be the case, since Kant had long promised to write a treatise on law and politics, and had written and lectured on natural law for decades before the revolution without publishing anything on it.[6] Yet as scholars point out, the

---

[4] Scholars seem to have missed the fact that Marx was specifically referencing the 1789 revolution. See Karl Marx, 'The Philosophical Manifesto of the Historical School of Law', in *Writings of the Young Marx on Philosophy and Society*, translated and edited by Loyd Easton and Kurt Guddat (Indianapolis, IN: Hackett Publishing Company, 1997), pp. 96–106, p. 100. Different versions of the claim were common among Kant's supporters during the 1790s. The claim was popularised by Heine and, according to Michael Morris, it dominated interpretations of Kantian philosophy during the first part of the nineteenth century. Morris, 'The French Revolution and the New School of Europe: Towards a Political Interpretation of German Idealism', in *European Journal of Philosophy*. 19, no. 4 (2011): 532–60.

[5] Paul Schrecker, 'Kant et la Révolution Française', in *Revue Philosophique de la France et de l'Étranger*, 128, no. 9/12 (1939): 394–426; Jacques Droz, *L'Allemagne et la Révolution française* (Paris: Presses Universitaires de France, 1949), p. 156; Ferenc Fehér, 'Practical Reason in the Revolution: Kant's Dialogue with the French Revolution', in *The French Revolution and the Birth of Modernity*, edited by Ferenc Fehér (Berkeley: University of California Press, 1990), pp. 201–18; and André Tosel, *Kant révolutionnaire. Droit et politique, suivi de textes choisis de là Doctrine du droit*, traduits par J.-P. Lefebvre (Paris: P.U.F., 1988).

[6] Peter Burg, *Kant und die Französische Revolution* (Berlin: Duncker und Humblot, 1974). Christian Ritter has tracked the incremental development of Kant's legal and political philosophy in *Der Rechtsgedanke Kants nach den frühen Quellen* (Frankfurt: V. Klostermann, 1971).

revolution inspired him.[7] He defined the citizen with the term *Citoyen*, and added a property qualification for the franchise, closely following those adopted in France in 1789 (TP 8: 295). When defending the sovereign's authority to repeal the hereditary property rights of the nobility and the clergy once public opinion ceased to favour them, he defended some of the most momentous policies the National Constituent Assembly took to dismantle the *ancien regime* (MM 6: 324). When Kant argued that republics are more peaceful, since rulers will be unable to wage war if they need the consent of the people who bear the financial and military burden of war (TPP 8:350), he was echoing a sentiment voiced by Jean Francois Reubell, the deputy of the Third Estate, who blamed wars on dynastic pacts and unaccountable rulers who start wars 'without the nation's consent but at the cost of the nation's blood and the nation's gold'.[8] In such instances, Kant adopted the revolution's policies and institutions and sought to provide the principles for them.

Rather than merely reacting to the revolution or developing his principles in isolation from it, Kant seems to have developed his legal and political philosophy through a process of reflective equilibrium, moving between legal and political practice in France and the principles he had deduced a priori (aided by his deep knowledge of the natural law tradition, in particular the writings of Achenwall, Rousseau, and Hobbes). The approach recalls his *Groundwork of The Metaphysics of Morals*, which assumes that ordinary cognition has an intuitive grasp of morals, tasking philosophy with providing the a priori principles (4: 392). Apologising for the undeveloped state of his sections on public right, he wrote that the topic is 'currently subject to so much discussion, and still so important, that they can well justify postponing a decisive judgment for some time' (MM 6: 209). Kant was an avid follower of these debates. No doubt he was thinking of people like himself when noting that 'in this crisis of the metamorphosis of the French state', the enlightened man is 'desperate to know the situation with his impatient and ardent desire for newspapers as the

---

[7] Karl Vorländer's early contribution highlighted Kant's critique of the nobility, of the established church, and his restriction of citizen rights. Many have identified the influence of Sieyès. According to Fehér and Gareth Stedman Jones, he influenced Kant's separation of powers and defence of constitutional monarchy, and according to Ingeborg Maus and Ulrich Thiele Sieyès inspired Kant's belief in the people as the *Pouvoir Constituant*. Karl Vorländer, 'Kants Stellung zur Französischen Revolution', in *Philosophische Abhandlungen* (Berlin: Verlag Bruno Cassirer, 1912), pp. 247–69; Fehér, 'Practical Reason in the Revolution'; Stedman Jones, 'Kant, the French Revolution and the Definition of the Republic', in *The Invention of the Modern Republic*, edited by Biancamaria Fontana (Cambridge: Cambridge University Press, 1994), pp. 154–72; Maus, *Zur Aufklärung der Demokratietheorie: Rechts – und demokratietheoretische Überlegungen im Anschluß an Kant* (Frankfurt: Suhrkamp, 1992); Thiele, *Repräsentation und Autonomieprinzip: Kants Demokratiekritik und ihre Hintergründe* (Berlin: Duncker & Humblot, 2003).

[8] Cited in Tim Blanning, *The Pursuit of Glory: Europe, 1648–1815* (London: Penguin books, 2007), p. 617.

raw material for highly interesting social conversations' (Drafts 19: 604). His own writings were part of that conversation, since he published in journals with wide audiences so that his essays could be immediately evaluated and discussed by contemporaries (Corr 12: 221).

Kant saw the parallel between the political event and his own philosophy early on. In a 1789 footnote to *Critique of the Power of Judgment*, he referred to 'a recently undertaken fundamental transformation of a great people into a state', a body politic where 'each member should certainly be not merely a means, but at the same time also an end, and, insofar as it contributes to the possibility of the whole, its position and function should also be determined by the idea of the whole' (5: 375). This shows he believed the 1789 revolutionaries were following the basic principle of always treating persons as ends in them-selves, and may also allude to Rousseau's notion of the general will as the state's governing principle. Kant and the French Revolutionaries shared a foundation in Rousseau's principles of equality and popular sovereignty. Emmanuel Joseph Sieyès – deputy to the Third Estate and chief ideologue behind the 1789 events – nonetheless rejected the imperative of popular assemblies, a corollary of Rousseau's conviction that sovereignty could not be represented.[9] Since a popular assembly was not an option in a republic of 30 million people, Sieyès sought to define how the nation could act as the sovereign through representatives. Kant engaged in the same endeavour in parallel.

Kant's admiration was not one-sided: some actors on the French stage took a fleeting interest in him. In February 1796 Karl Théremin, a Prussian diplomat in Paris and member of Sieyès's circle, attempted to arrange a correspondence between the two.[10] This was prompted by the publication of Kant's *Toward Perpetual Peace*, from 1795, which itself was inspired by the peace treaty between France and Prussia. His defence of republican government reads like a vindication of the 1789 French liberals. Like them, Kant defended individual freedom, commercial enterprise, meritocracy, legal equality, the end of heredi-tary privilege, popular sovereignty, constitutional monarchy, and the separation of powers. For the 1789 liberals (unlike the leaders of the English Glorious Revolution a century before), the revolution did more than depose a bad ruler; it fundamentally transformed a stagnant late feudal society. Théremin saw Kant's philosophy as a 'complement to the revolution',[11] and there were rumours in

---

[9] Jean-Jacques Rousseau, *On the Social Contract,* in *The Basic Political Writings of Jean-Jacques Rousseau,* edited by Donald A. Cress (Indianapolis, IN, and Cambridge: Hackett Publishing Company, 1987), book 3, chapter 15.

[10] Schrecker, 'Kant et la Révolution Française', p. 408.

[11] Karl Théremin, letter to his brother of 2 January 1796 (12: 59), in Immanuel Kant, *Briefwechsel, Band III, 1795-1803,* in *Kant's gesammelte Schriften* vol. 12 (Berlin: W. de Gruyter, 1922), p. 59.

Berlin – which Kant had to publicly deny – that he had been invited to be the new legislator of France.[12] Konrad Engelbert Oelsner, a German publicist, wrote the following in the introduction to his 1796 German translation of Sieyès's political writings (expressing a perhaps unhealthy infatuation with great men):

> The two most outstanding thinkers now living, Sieyès and Kant, setting out from opposite points, met at the same goal. Sieyès through a posteriori synthesis, and Kant through a priori analysis, unite in a stirring and inestimable practical result that destroys despotism forever and founds an eternally perfectible freedom. Man, they say, is never a mere means of society, still less of princes; he is an end to himself.[13]

Kant admitted to being honoured by the attention of the 'famous' and 'commendable' Sieyès, but the exchange of letters never took place because he thought it inappropriate to meddle in the politics of another country.[14] Although he did not draft any laws for France, he did suggest that his books be translated into French. He also tried to persuade Prussian authorities that they had nothing to fear and everything to gain from a republican France since republics tend to be peaceful (CF 7: 86–7). They should not consider sympathisers (like his own followers) enemies of the state. Although it is strange that Kant said almost nothing about the Jacobin dictatorship and terror during 1792–4, one of the most remarkable political experiments of Western history,[15] his basic principles can be read as an explicit rejection of their attempt to foster virtue through terror, to implement direct democracy, and use law for political ends.[16]

Kant's support for the people's role in politics was not a response to the revolution but dates back to the mid 1760s, around the time he read Rousseau and started teaching Achenwall's natural law theory, which he did on twelve occasions until 1788.[17] His shorter political essays in the 1780s had developed

---

[12] Alain Ruiz, 'Neues über Kant und Sieyès. Ein unbekannter Brief des Philosophen an Anton Ludwig Théremin' (März 1796)', in *Kant-Studien* 68, no. 4 (1977): 446–53, 450.

[13] Oelsner, quoted by Isaac Nakhimovsky in *The Closed Commercial State: Perpetual Peace and Commercial Society from Rousseau to Fichte* (Princeton: Princeton University Press, 2011), p. 24.

[14] Ruiz, 'Neues über Kant', 450. See also Jachman's biography of Kant in *Immanuel Kant in Rede und Gespräch*, edited by Rudolf Malter (Hamburg: Felix Meiner, 1990), pp. 349–50.

[15] One exception is a remark criticising Danton's commitment to direct democracy (TP 8: 302). See Gianluca Sadun Bordoni, 'Kant and Danton', in *Kant-Studien* 111, no. 3 (2020): 503–9.

[16] Jacob Rogozinski develops this view in 'Un crime inexpiable (Kant et le régicide)', in *Rue Descartes*, no. 4 (1992): 99–120.

[17] See for example the following remarks: 6594, 7548, 7969 (Refl 19: 100, 452, 567). Achenwall considered that public command originally belonged to the people through the social contract. See *Iuris naturalis pars posterior complectens jus familiae, jus publicum, et jus gentium*, published in Göttingen in 1763 and reprinted in Immanuel Kant, *Kant's handschriftlicher*

a teleological view of history, which proposed universal republicanism as its inevitable end point. His lectures on natural law during the 1780s had included more extensive defences of popular sovereignty, defining it as a system that grounds legal justice in the voice of all in an ideal original contract (L-NR 27: 1382). Frederick II's relaxation of censorship, which opened up public debate on political matters and led to a groundswell of journals and newspapers, put the question of the people's role in politics at the centre of public debates about the relationship between enlightenment and revolution.[18] Kant applauded that development and advised rulers that they had everything to gain by consulting an enlightened population on legislation, and nothing to fear as long as they had a 'well-disciplined and numerous army ready to guarantee public peace' (WIE 8: 41).

The French Revolution cast that debate in a new light. Although German public opinion had generally welcomed the revolution, the trial and execution of Louis XVI made it look like a failed experiment that seemed to confirm the old fear that enlightenment foments rebellion.[19] Conservatives like Justus Möser, August Wilhelm Rehberg, and Friedrich Gentz came out strongly against Kant's idealism. They argued that grounding principles in reason – in abstract principles of human rights – made individuals the arbiters of right and wrong, and challenged all the existing conventions of society, which the conservatives considered legitimate ancient rights and bulwarks against anarchy. The brute masses (*rohe Haufen*), Rehberg wrote, had nothing to lose by tearing down existing institutions and were driven to do so by a blind fury generated by the Enlightenment's 'abstract' ideals.[20] Gentz was probably referring to Kant when he wrote, 'the philosopher creates systems; the rabble forges murderous weapons from them'.[21] Johann Heinrich Tieftrunk, a moderate Kantian, came to his defence and claimed that Kant's definition of enlightenment as the courage to think for oneself actually gives a more solid foundation for the state and

---

Nachlass. Band VI, Moralphilosophie, Rechtsphilosophie und Religionsphilosophie, in *Kant's gesammelte Schriften*, vol. 19 (Berlin: De Gruyter, 1971), pp. 325–442, at §§ 95, 97, 158. See also Ritter, *Der Rechtsgedanke Kants*, p. 247ff.

[18] Several of these contributions can be found in Zwi Batscha (ed.), *Aufklärung und Gedankenfreiheit: 15 Anregungen, aus der Geschichte zu lernen* (Frankfurt: Suhrkamp, 1977), and James Schmidt (ed.), *What Is Enlightenment? Eighteenth-Century Answers and Twentieth-Century Questions* (Berkeley: University of California Press, 1996).

[19] George Peabody Gooch, *Germany and the French Revolution* (New York: Russel & Russel, 1966); Droz, *L'Allemagne et la Révolution française*; Rudolf Vierhaus, 'Politisches Bewusstsein in Deutschland vor 1789', in *Der Staat* 6 (1967): 175–96.

[20] August Wilhelm Rehberg, *Untersuchungen über die französische Revolution nebst kritischen Nachrichten von den merkwürdigen Schriften welche darüber in Frankreich erschienen sind, Zweyter Theil* (Hannover, Osnabrück: Christian Ritscher, 1793), pp. 78, and 21.

[21] Quoted by Ursula Vogel in *Konservative Kritik an der Bürgerlichen Revolution* (Darmstadt and Neuwied: Luchterhand, 1972), p. 90. My translation.

religious authority because it teaches subjects the *reasons* why they should honour God and the government.[22] Indeed it was *lack* of enlightenment that caused the French to rebel: moved by passion, they were enthralled by the philosophy of one man (Rousseau) and incapable of thinking for themselves. Kant would certainly agree with his follower. Rebellion, as Kant came to argue during the 1790s, tends to be triggered by criminal rulers and bad constitutions that 'reduce the people to despair and hence to rebellion' (TPP 8: 375, 372; MM 6: 330; CF 7: 80). Ordinary people are fundamentally capable of rational agency and will rebel if subjected to power beyond reason (TP 8: 306).[23]

The events of 1789 and 1792 exemplify, respectively, legitimate and illegitimate political transitions. The first – an orderly transfer of sovereignty to the people – resulted in the establishment of a constitutional monarchy, whereas the second was a mob rebellion that led to a regicide and the destruction of the state's unity. Comparing the 'two revolutions' highlights Kant's distinction between a political, yet legitimate, constitutional transition, and a transition that was mere political justice. In the French Revolution, the people entered the stage of history, successfully at first, and disastrously in the second instance. Kant viewed the sequence of events as a strong moral warning against political change untethered by procedural constraints, no matter how appealing its ends.

Kant's discussion of the French Revolution foreshadows modern discussions of transitional justice: the normative deliberations regarding what regime change permits and requires, and which procedures should apply to leaders of the old regime. Kant's *legalistic* claim about transitional justice distinguishes his position from scholars like Judith Shklar and Michael Walzer, who argue that highly imperfect judicial procedures can be justified if they can secure confidence in the new regime. 'Revolutionary justice is defensible whenever it points the way to everyday justice', Walzer wrote.[24] Illegal actions can be legitimate if they accord with a greater good. Kant's reasoning rejects that kind of argument: principles of justice should never be compromised or

---

[22] Johann Heinrich Tieftrunk, 'Über den Einfluß der Aufklärung auf Revolutionen', in *Aufklärung und Gedankenfreiheit: 15 Anregungen, aus der Geschichte zu lernen*, edited by Zwi Batscha (Frankfurt: Suhrkamp, 1977), p. 196.

[23] Kant also employed cultural explanations, mentioning as a characteristic of the French nation an 'infectious *spirit of freedom*, which probably also pulls reason itself into its play, and, in the relations of the people to the state, causes an enthusiasm that shakes everything and goes beyond all bounds', in his *Anthropology*, published in 1798 (7: 314). The phlegmatic and obedient Germans, by contrast, 'would rather submit to despotism than get mixed up in innovations (especially unauthorized reforms in government)'. Kant's discussions of 1789 and 1792 do not depend on these stereotypes, however.

[24] Michael Walzer, *Regicide and Revolution: Speeches at the Trial of Louis XVI* (New York: Columbia University Press, 1993), p. 79.

instrumentalised for the sake of future political ends, even laudable ones such as the foundation of a republic. His claim is based on the imperative of respecting the legal structure governing the interactions of individuals, not on a consequentialist rejection of the empirical uncertainty that inevitably follows the manipulation of outcomes for ulterior motives.

But exactly what does that mean in practice? Although some consider Kant disengaged from practical questions, his detailed discussions of the two great transitions of the French Revolution is evidence to the contrary, providing a glimpse of his ideas about theory and practice, and providing a fresh perspective on a founding moment of Western history. The first section of this Element presents Kant's philosophical principles, and the second and third sections analyse how he applied these principles to the events in 1789 and 1792 respectively.

2 Philosophical Foundations

For Kant, the French Revolution was fundamentally about a nation's right to establish a republican constitution (CF 7: 85). This was a goal he endorsed, yet since Kant's commitment to popular sovereignty is not immediately obvious, this section discusses the foundations of the theory he developed to interpret events in France. His critics often consider Kant's commitment to popular sovereignty as merely to the doctrine as an idea, while in practice he was quite content to support autocracy.[25] After all, he saw the original contract not as an actual historical occurrence, but as an idea of justice, whose principles are independent of electoral processes. Moreover, his rejection of any right of resistance and revolution is sometimes taken as evidence that he prioritised order over justice, 'sacralizing the status quo'.[26] Kant's well-known Hobbesian claim that 'The human being is an animal which, when it lives among others of its species, has need of a master' (IUH 8: 23) seems to mean that he thought individual liberty should be subordinated to the forces of order, and that people were incapable of collective democratic organisation. His critics surmise that Kant only cared about the inner freedom of the individual, which can be realised perfectly well under authoritarian conditions.[27] Yet, as many Kant scholars

---

[25] Hella Mandt, 'Historisch-politische Traditionselemente im politischen Denken Kants', in *Materialen zu Kants Rechtsphilosophie*, edited by Zwi Batscha (Frankfurt: Suhrkamp, 1976); Philip Pettit, 'Two Republican Traditions', in *Republican Democracy: Liberty, Law and Politics*, edited by Andreas Niederberger and Philipp Schink (Edinburgh: Edinburgh University Press, 2014), pp. 169–204; Stedman Jones, 'Kant, the French Revolution and the Definition of the Republic'; Richard Tuck, *The Rights of War and Peace: Political Thought and the International Order from Grotius to Kant* (Oxford: Oxford University Press, 1999), p. 211.

[26] Pettit, 'Two Republican Traditions'.

[27] Stedman Jones maintains this view, in an article remarkable for the lack of a single reference to *The Metaphysics of Morals*. His interpretation seems to rely on Leonard Krieger's post war book on the *German Idea of Freedom*, which posits a continuity in the German attitude to freedom

today emphasise, he was deeply committed to the ideal of equal liberty and undeniably defended a republicanism of elected governments accountable to their citizens.[28] The next section supports that scholarship, discussing the principle of freedom and the institutional structures that were central to Kant's thought and that grounded his analysis of the transfer of sovereignty during the spring of 1789. This section is followed by a discussion of his theory of obligation to the state, and his rejection of a right of revolution, which grounds his analysis of the 1792 revolution.

2.1 Right, Popular Sovereignty, and Reform

The claim that Kant cared more about inner moral autonomy than external freedom is plausible only if we accept that his moral writings override his principles of right. The problem is that Kant left no evidence of any such preference ranking. Indeed, *The Metaphysics of Morals* demonstrates that they operate in co-equal dimensions. He divides the moral domain into juridical laws, which are backed by coercion, and ethical laws, which require a specific motivation: doing the right thing for the right reason, out of respect for duty (MM 6: 218). Ethical laws cannot be coercively enforced because they concern the justification of actions, rather than the actions themselves. By contrast, in the legal and political dimensions, duties can be discharged out of prudence, self-interest, habit, and so on, and not necessarily out of respect for the law. Kant refers to juridical laws as 'right', or *Recht* in German. The universal principle of right allows people to distinguish right from wrong:

> Any action is right if it can coexist with everyone's freedom in accordance with a universal law, or if on its maxim the freedom of choice of each can coexist with everyone's freedom in accordance with a universal law. (MM 6: 230)

This is a purely formal, not a material, principle (TPP 8: 377). It does not concern our ends, but the compatibility of our choices in achieving those ends. A basic egalitarianism, which assumes an equal right to freedom and contradicts the system of privileges and inherited social status characterising the *ancien*

---

from Luther on, characterised by 'secular submission and spiritual independence'. Diethelm Klippel offered a thorough analysis and rebuttal of such views, which are associated with the frequently criticised notion of a German *Sonderweg*. See Stedman Jones, 'Kant, the French Revolution and the Definition of the Republic'; Krieger, *The German Idea of Freedom: History of a Political Tradition* (Boston, MA: Beacon Press, 1957), pp. 45, 49; and Klippel, 'Politische Theorien in Deutschland des 18. Jahrhunderts', in *Aufklärung* 2 (1988): 57–88.

[28] Maus, *Zur Aufklärung der Demokratietheorie*; Arthur Ripstein, *Force and Freedom: Kant's Legal and Political Philosophy* (Cambridge, MA: Harvard University Press, 2009); Sharon Byrd and Joachim Hruschka, *Kant's Doctrine of Right: A Commentary* (Cambridge: Cambridge University Press, 2010).

regime, underlies this claim. Kant defines freedom as 'independence from being constrained by another's choice', and as an innate right (MM 6: 237). It implies that persons may not be made the subjects of others, as is the case with enslavement or paternalistic treatment by a master. They must be free to set and pursue their own goals, so long as their choices are compatible with the choices of everyone else. It follows that there can be no innate inequalities among humans, such as there are in a hereditary aristocracy. The intrinsic right to freedom is the basis, the moral foundation, of all individuals can acquire.

The claim that Kant's constitution is designed to curb natural human drives so citizens can develop moral virtue assumes that the state's main contribution is to establish a master, who can secure order, enabling individual moral agency. That interpretation may be understandable if one mistakes Kant's teleological writings from the 1780s as his theory of right, yet it would be to render the constitution merely an instrument, and that is certainly not Kant's view. The purpose of the state, as Arthur Ripstein has argued, is to secure freedom as independence by solving problems that arise when individuals seek to claim rights in the state of nature.[29] Chief among these problems is determining from an omnilateral view what is right and wrong. Individuals may unilaterally claim to have a right to certain things, but without a legislator to determine laws for right and wrong, an executive to protect the rights, and a judiciary to decide in disputes, there is no conclusive way of determining individual rights. Kant's postulate of public right therefore states that those who unavoidably live side by side with others are under an obligation to leave the state of nature (MM 6: 307). Thus, the purpose of the state is not to keep selfish and mean inclinations in check (so that persons gradually can be educated morally), but to render justice in an objective way. A ruler that merely established order without rightful law would not succeed in establishing freedom, which is the state's source of legitimacy, its right to rule. In fact, a merely repressive regime would not on that view count as a civil condition, which is defined in legal terms as 'a union of a multitude of human beings under laws of right' (MM 6: 313).

While Kant works within the social contract tradition, he thinks the contract is merely '*an idea* of reason' and not an actual event (TP 297; MM 6: 315). One may think that betrays an undemocratic tendency to substitute actual participation for mere ideals, yet, as we shall see, Kant derives from the idea of the original contract the notion that the people are the ultimate authority in the state. To Kant, the original contract functions as a standard of justice, which is based on the idea that a law or policy is not unjust if it is conceivable that everyone could agree to it. To be subject only to law to which one could consent is, for

---

[29] Ripstein, *Force and Freedom*, p. 14ff.

Kant, to be free, according to the idea of *volenti non fit iniuria* ('no wrong is done to someone who consents') (MM 6: 314; Drafts 23: 347).[30] Kant's notion of a 'general will' formulates the standard of justice, which legislators then use as a touchstone to enact positive laws. The people's general united will must be *represented* by institutions, which he therefore refers to as sovereign.

The general will must not inherently be established through democratic institutions, by contrast to Rousseau. The united will of the people (*der Volkswille*) is instead represented by public legal authority, what Kant calls the 'pure idea of the head of state (*Staatsoberhaupt*)', or the sovereign (*der Souverän*) (MM 6: 338). We need to consider Kant's concept of sovereignty in more detail. For Kant, sovereignty is the possession of ultimate political authority. The sovereign (*der Souverän*, or *Staatsoberhaupt*) has ultimate authority in establishing and enforcing the laws of the community (MM 6: 338). It is due to this service that there always is a final official answer on right, and an assurance that it will be protected. Kant's usage of the term can be a bit confusing because he uses it for two different entities. On the one hand, he speaks of the *united* public authority as the sovereign, comprising the three authorities of the state – the legislative, executive, and judiciary (MM 6: 338). This is because subjects face them as the united 'head of a state' sometimes in the capacity of legislator, other times in the capacity of enforcer or judge.

Yet, Kant also speaks of just *one* of the three authorities as the sovereign, and that is the legislator: the *gesetzgebende Oberhaupt des Staats* (MM 6: 320) and the *oberste gesetzgebende Macht* (TPP 8: 299). This is because within these three powers there is a hierarchy, where legislation is the highest power, and foundational (like the major premise in a practical syllogism, in Kant's terms MM 6: 314). The legislative power delegates authority to the executive power, which Kant also refers to as the government (*Regierung*), the *Regent* (MM 6: 317), and the head of public administration (*das Oberhaupt der Staatsverwaltung*, TP 8: 294). Since the government's authority is delegated from the sovereign legislative authority, the sovereign 'can also take the ruler's authority away from him, depose him, or reform his administration' (MM 6: 317). Thus, because the government is the agent, or organ, of the legislator, tasked with enforcing the law, Kant is correct to sometimes describe it as the sovereign because it is part of a system of public authority that represents the

---

[30] 'Now when someone makes arrangements about another, it is always possible for him to do the other wrong; but he can never do wrong in what he decides upon with regard to himself (for *volenti nonfit iniuria*). Therefore only the concurring and united will of all, insofar as each decides the same thing for all and all for each, and so only the general united will of the people, can be legislative' (MM 6: 314).

sovereign's will, even though technically the legislature has supreme authority (TP 8: 302; MM 6: 317, 319).

It is one thing to establish the idea of the sovereign, but another to designate who is to be sovereign. The notional head of state can only be effective on the people's will if it is represented by one or several physical human beings that are in command. Using a traditional distinction, Kant writes that that task can either be performed by one, by several equals, or by all together, leading to three different forms of state (*forma imperii*) with three different sovereigns: autocratic, aristocratic, and democratic (TPP 8: 352; MM 6: 339). The sovereign represents the united will of the people, not the wills of the individuals understood distributively. Kant's idea is similar to Hobbes's idea that the sovereign represents the person of the state (the *persona civitatis*), not the multitude of actual persons and estates. As Quentin Skinner has argued, for Hobbes, the multitude is seen as having authorised the Hobbesian sovereign in a covenant to 'carry' the person of the state, and the multitude by this act of representation becomes unified as a people.[31]

The three types of sovereignty can be combined with either of two forms of government (*forma regiminis*). The first type of government is republicanism, which entails the constitutional separation of legislative and executive powers. That separation establishes government by law rather than by decree. Since legislators do not apply the law, they must draft and promulgate laws of general application rather than laws directed towards particular political ends.

> Republicanism is the political principle of separation of the executive power (the government) from the legislative power; despotism is that of the high-handed management of the state by laws the regent has himself given, inasmuch as he handles the public will as his private will. (TPP 8: 352)

Despotism, the form of government in which the head of state controls both the legislative and executive, is the opposite of republicanism. The democratic form of state, which Kant thinks of as a form of direct democracy, is despotic because it expresses the arbitrary will of a majority, and therefore does not represent the

---

[31] Quentin Skinner, 'Hobbes and the Purely Artificial Person of the State', in *The Journal of Political Philosophy* 7, no. 1 (1999): 21. This similarity led Richard Tuck to conclude that for Kant, 'a single-person legislator [is] quite possible and even desirable on the ground of simplicity'. See *The Rights of War and Peace*, p. 211. But Tuck neglects to mention that Kant, in the same paragraph, proceeds to write the following: 'It is true that, with regard to the administration of right within a state, the simplest form [autocracy] is also the best. With regard to right itself, however, this form of state is the most dangerous for a people, in view of how conducive it is to despotism' (MM 6: 339). As if to drive home the point, Kant adds a tacit quotation from Alexander Pope's lines: 'For forms of government let fools contest / whate'er is best administer'd is best', which he rejects out of hand as false. Kant associated this sentiment with the royalist and anti-revolutionary Jacques Mallet du Pan (1749–1800), who, as Kant reported in *Perpetual Peace*, had taken it as his motto (8: 353).

people's united will, and it is not limited by a constitution since the expressed popular will is always prior to laws (Refl 19: 595). Even monarchy is better than democracy because, theoretically at least, a monarch can represent the united general will (TPP 8: 352).

The republican constitution is 'lawful freedom', which Kant describes as a citizen's 'attitude of obeying no other law than that to which he has given his consent' (MM 6: 314). This translates into a right to choose representatives (*Repräsentanten*) (TP 8: 295–6; MM 6: 317; Drafts 23: 342), meaning the people act 'through' elected officials.[32] This allowed Kant to (famously) deduce that republics are less prone to declare war because citizens, who have to bear the burden of war, are less likely than unaccountable princes to start one.[33] Kant limits the franchise to property owners (TP 8: 295–296, 23: 136; Refl 19: 568), apparently following developments in France.[34] He based this restriction on a republican rationale: only those who own some property, are independent, and '*serves* no one other than the commonwealth'.

Although all governments result from conquest and usurpation, they can eventually work themselves clean, and sovereigns are obliged to reform society in the image of a true republic (MM 6: 340; CF 7: 91). *The Metaphysics of Morals* uses terms from biology to distinguish between two kinds of transformative political action.[35] The first is *metamorphosis*: the transformation (*Veränderung*) of a constitution through legislation, which allows the state to continue in existence (MM 6: 340). The second is *palingenesis*: a new beginning after an insurrection in which the people acting as a mob have overthrown the civil constitution and returned society to the state of nature. Needless to say, Kant defended metamorphosis. He saw the 1789 constitutional change as a metamorphosis, and the rebellion and introduction of the republic in 1792 as a palingenesis.

The original contract obliges the sovereign to align the constitution with the legal form of a republican constitution, which entails establishing separate legislative and executive branches of government (TPP 8: 350; MM 6: 340, 264). The sovereign has no discretion to change the constitutional form itself (democratic, aristocratic, or autocratic), though. As Kant says, 'For even if the sovereign decided to transform

---

[32] 'Any true republic is and can only be a system of representing the people [*ein repräsentatives System des Volks*], in order to protect its rights in its name, by all the citizens acting through [*durch*] their delegates' (MM 6: 341).

[33] 'For they must always be regarded as co-legislating members of a state (not merely as means, but also as ends in themselves), and must therefore give their free assent, through their representatives, not only to waging war in general but also to each particular declaration of war' (MM 6: 346, cf. TPP 8: 350, CF 7: 91).

[34] Malcolm Crook, *Elections in the French Revolution: An Apprenticeship in Democracy, 1789–99* (Cambridge: Cambridge University Press, 1996).

[35] Howard Williams has traced the origins of this view in *Kant's Critique of Hobbes: Sovereignty and Cosmopolitanism* (Cardiff: University of Wales Press, 2003).

itself into a democracy, it could still do the people a wrong, since the people itself could abhor such a constitution and find one of the other forms more to its advantage' (MM 6: 340). The sovereign should recuse himself and let the people decide the new form of sovereignty in some sort of constitutional convention. The reason for this is Kant's belief in popular sovereignty as the foundation of the original contract, and therefore as not bound by pre-existing law: 'For in it (the people) is originally found the supreme authority from which all rights of individuals as mere subjects (and in any event as officials of the state) must be derived' (MM 6: 340; Refl 19: 567). Ingeborg Maus has argued that Kant was inspired by Sieyès's idea of the nation as the *pouvoir constituant*, the source of legitimacy for any established legal order.[36] However, Achenwall also supported the notion of the people as the originary power behind the constitution, free to re-make the constitution (once the contract of subjection had been broken).[37]

Kant argued that the state must be reformed '*from top to bottom*', meaning that since reform must come through established legal channels, it is formally the task of the government (CF 7: 92). The obligation to introduce a republican constitution is conditional on it not weakening the state by exposing it to powerful neighbours or internal breakdown and anarchy (TPP 8: 374). Anarchy could result from subjects using their freedom to subvert the civil, political, religious, and military order. To ensure that a reform does not destabilise society, Kant devised the notion of a 'permissive law', which scholars of transitional justice often see as a pragmatic way of balancing reform with respect for principles.[38] The 'permissive law' allows an unjust constitution to remain in place in cases where 'premature' liberalisation would lead to anarchy (TPP 8: 373; Refl 19: 604).[39] Yet Kant also insisted that people cannot 'ripen to freedom' unless they actually have it:

> 'I admit that I am not comfortable with this way of speaking, which even clever men are wont to use: A certain people (intent on establishing civil freedom) is not ripe for freedom'; 'The bondmen of a landed proprietor are not yet ripe for

---

[36] Ingeborg Maus, *Zur Aufklärung der Demokratietheorie*, p. 79ff.

[37] Gottfried Achenwall, 'Iuris naturalis pars posterior complectens jus familiae, jus publicum, et jus gentium (Göttingen, 1763)', in Immanuel Kant, *Gesammelte Schriften*, vol. 19 (Berlin: Georg Reimer, 1934) 325–442, §§ 95; 158.

[38] See Elisabeth Ellis, *Kant's Politics: Provisional Theory for an Uncertain World* (New Haven, CT: Yale University Press, 2005); Robert S. Taylor, 'Democratic Transitions and the Progress of Absolutism in Kant's Political Thought', in *Journal of Politics* 68, no. 3 (2006): 556–70. Reinhard Brandt made an early contribution to this literature: see 'Das Problem der Erlaubnisgesetze im Spätwerk Kants', in Otfried Höffe (ed.), *Immanuel Kant: Zum Ewigen Frieden* (Berlin: Akademie Verlag, 1995), pp. 69–86, p. 79ff. See also Robert Spaeman, 'Kants Kritik der Widerstandsrechts', in *Materialen zu Kants Rechtsphilosophie*, edited by Zwi Batscha (Frankfurt: Suhrkamp, 1976), pp. 347–58.

[39] Kant was clearly thinking of Prussia, warning that the people should not start a revolution there, since the monarchy was probably the only way the country could survive surrounded by

freedom'; and so too, 'People are in general not yet ripe for freedom of belief.'
For on this assumption freedom will never come, since we cannot ripen to it if we
are not already established in it (we must be free in order to be able to make use of
our powers purposively in freedom). (MM 6: 190)[40]

Thus, any reform leading to a republic will inevitably result in some
abuses of freedom. That argument was written in 1793, at a time when
the French Revolution had already resulted in significant abuses of
freedom, and may have been a response to conservatives who interpreted
the French Revolution as evidence that humans are incapable of political
freedom.[41]

2.2 Resistance and Revolution

Kant's arguments about the 1792 rebellion against Louis XVI, and the
subsequent trial and execution of the king, are based on his rejection of
a right of resistance and revolution. The principles, which are incorporated
in all his post-1792 writings, were not inspired by the events in France but
can be traced back to his 1760s lectures on Achenwall's natural law theory,
which defended a view of sovereignty that excludes a right to judge the ruler
(L-NR 27: 1319–94). Kant's total rejection of a right of revolution and
resistance has generated a large critical literature, since it implies that
tyrannical regimes are legitimate. Critics often assume that a right of resistance and revolution is inherent in democratic rule, a premise whose paradig-
matic formulations can be traced to thinkers such as John Locke and Thomas
Paine.[42] Many have argued that Kant's rejection of a legal right of resistance
to the state does not exclude the possibility of a *moral* right against the state,

---

powerful European neighbours. Nor should Prussia intervene in France, since the republican
constitution itself would render that country a more peaceful neighbour (CF 7: 86; TPP 8: 373).

[40] Kant may have changed his mind on this score since writing 'What is Enlightenment?' (1785),
which defended restrictions on civil freedom (while encouraging commerce, the public sphere,
and education) so that subjects could mature into citizens (WIE 8: 42). Yet, the later text may also
just add a nuance.

[41] Indeed, the 'clever men' may have been the 'men of practice' Kant debated in the 1790s. The
conservatives Rehberg, Gentz, and Möser argued that people are too irrational and short-sighted
to govern themselves, and that a republic with self-legislating citizens would require a nation of
gods. Rulers should deal with subjects prudentially, as minors, and not from a principle of justice
but from a principle of order. Kant responded that the conservatives themselves produce the
trouble they predict because, treated as incapable of freedom, subjects may come to think of
themselves as 'the most miserable of all beings in the world' and therefore indeed incapable of
independence (TPP 8: 378). Subjects may even be driven to rebellion: 'the people may also try
out its own force and thus make every lawful constitution insecure' (TP 8: 306; CF 7: 80).

[42] Pettit, 'Two Republican Traditions'. For a contrasting view, see Katrin Flikschuh, 'Reason,
Right, and Revolution: Kant and Locke', in *Philosophy & Public Affairs* 36, no. 4 (2008):
375–404.

based on Kant's principle of right, the categorical imperative, or the principle of virtue.[43] The problem with that argument is Kant's conviction that all claims to right in a civil condition must be enacted in positive law (Refl 19: 565). Others, accepting this premise, have argued that when rulers use force beyond law, the condition ceases to be that of a state and becomes what Kant termed barbarism. Society then reverts to a state of nature, where a provisional right entitles persons to coerce others into creating a new constitution. This was the argumentative strategy of Kant's followers in the 1790s,[44] and it is currently dominant in the literature.[45]

Exploring Kant's argument can help us understand his verdict on the 1792 rebellion. The main terms he uses are resistance (*Widersetzlichkeit*), insurrection (*Aufstand, Aufruhr*), and rebellion (*Rebellion*) (TP 8: 301ff).[46] These were traditionally pejorative terms used to describe political disobedience to government. Unlike revolution, though, they did not necessarily entail constitutional change. Kant occasionally uses the term revolution, by which he means 'a violent overthrow of an already existing defective constitution''' where there is

---

[43] Werner Haensel, *Kant's Lehre vom Widerstandsrecht: Ein Beitrag zur Systematik der Kantischen Rechtsphilosophie* (Berlin: Pan-Verlag Rolf Heis, 1926), pp. 56–7 and 69; Sarah Williams Holtman, 'Revolution, Contradiction, and Kantian Citizenship', in *Kant's Metaphysics of Morals: Interpretative Essays*, edited by Mark Timmons (Oxford: Oxford University Press, 2002), pp. 209–32, p. 227; Allen Rosen, *Kant's Theory of Justice* (Ithaca, NY: Cornell University Press, 1993), pp. 171–2; H. S. Reiss, 'Kant and the Right of Rebellion', in *Journal of the History of Ideas* 17 (1956): 190. Thomas E. Hill Jr., 'Questions About Kant's Opposition to Revolution', in *The Journal of Value Inquiry* 36 (2002): 294ff; Christine M. Korsgaard, 'Taking the Law into Our Own Hands: Kant on the Right to Revolution', in *Reclaiming the History of Philosophy: Essays for John Rawls*, edited by Christine Korsgaard, Andrews Reath, and Barbara Herman (Cambridge: Cambridge University Press, 1997).

[44] This argument was made by Ludwig Heinrich Jakob, Friedrich Schlegel, Karl Heinrich Heydenreich, Johann Adam Bergk, Johann Gottlieb Fichte, Johann Benjamin Erhard, and Johann Heinrich Tieftrunk. I have discussed this in *Kant's Politics in Context* (Oxford: Oxford University Press, 2014). Kant's followers may have been inspired by Rousseau, who had written about magistrates breaking the law that 'Once social compact is violated natural liberty is regained', but they may also have had in mind paragraph 16 of the *Declaration of the Rights of Man and the Citizen*, which proclaimed that a community where the separation of powers is not provided for and where rights are not secure lacks a constitution. The theory also played an important role to Aquinas, the Monarchomachs, Althusius, Grotius, and Locke, and its locus classicus is Augustine's trope that 'Kingdoms without justice are like criminal gangs'. See *On the Social Contract*, 1.6, p. 75; National Assembly of France, 'Declaration of the Rights of Man and the Citizen', in *Introduction to Contemporary Civilization in the West: A Source Book*, vol. 2, edited by Marvin Harris, Sidney Morgenbesser, Joseph Rothschild, and Bernard Wishy (New York: Columbia University Press, 1961), pp. 33–5, § 16; *City of God*, translated by Henry Bettenson (London: Penguin, 2003), pp. 139 and 882.

[45] See Domenico Losurdo, *Immanuel Kant: Freiheit, Recht und Revolution;* Maus, *Zur Aufklärung der Demokratietheorie;* Wolfgang Kersting, *Wohlgeordnete Freiheit: Immanuel Kants Rechts- und Staatsphilosophie* (Frankfurt: Suhrkamp, 1993); Ripstein, *Force and Freedom;* Byrd and Hruschka, *Kant's Doctrine of Right.*

[46] For further analysis of these concepts, see Peter Nicholson, 'Kant on the Duty Never to Resist the Sovereign', in *Ethics*, vol. 86, no. 3 (1976): 215.

an 'intervening moment' outside of any juridical condition (MM 6: 355; Refl 19: 592). Noting that in real life successful uprisings that lead to new constitutions are celebrated, Kant mentions the Dutch Revolt (1566–1648), the Swiss War of Independence (1648), and the English Glorious Revolution (1688).[47] The instigators of *failed* revolts, by contrast, are treated as political criminals. But, Kant argues, rather than letting the outcome of a revolution determine whether it was justified, we must analyse the principle behind uprisings and revolutions and ask whether it is compatible with the principle of right (TP 8: 301). Kant famously answered that question in the negative, since it follows from the idea of the civil constitution that the sovereign cannot be opposed, and from the postulate of public right that no one has the right to return society to the state of nature.

In making this argument, Kant was explicitly debating Achenwall, as well as several 'worthy men' who may have included Burke, Gentz, and Christian Garve.[48] As several scholars have pointed out, he is challenging the natural law tradition and its contract of subjection,[49] quoting the following section from Achenwall's *Iuris naturalis*:

> If the danger that threatens a commonwealth as a result of continuing to endure the injustice of the head of state is greater than the danger to be feared from taking up arms against him, then the people can resist him, for the sake of this right withdraw from its contract of subjection [*Unterwerfungsvertrag*], and dethrone him as a tyrant. (TP 8: 301)

Achenwall belonged to the Wolffian school, which had based the obligation to obey on the contract of subjection between the heads of households and the ruler. This contract bound the monarch to rule for the public good according to the basic laws.[50] In a lawful regime (*Gesetzmäßiges Reich, regnum legitimum*)

---

[47] Kant mentions several other rebellions and revolutions, including the Jacobite rising of 1745 (MM 6: 333) and the Brabant revolution of 1789. He may have had the Haitian revolution in mind when describing 'the Negroes on the Sugar Islands' being driven to despair by their master (MM 6: 330). Karl Ameriks has noted the puzzling absence of reflections on the American revolution in 'Kant and Dignity: Missed Connections with the United States', in *The Court of Reason Proceedings of the 13th International Kant Congress*, edited by Beatrix Himmelmann and Camilla Serck-Hanssen (Berlin: Walter de Gruyter GmbH, 2022), pp. 27–47.

[48] These views are held respectively by Paul Wittichen, 'Kant und Burke', in *Historische Zeitschrift* 93 (1904): 253–5; Therese Dietrich, 'Kant's Polemik mit dem absprechenden Ehrenmann Friedrich Gentz', in *Dialektik*, 17 (1989): 128–136, and Dieter Henrich, 'On the Meaning of Rational Action in the State', in *Kant and Political Philosophy: The Contemporary Legacy*, edited by Ronald Beiner and William James Booth (New Haven, CT: Yale University Press, 1993), pp. 96–116. For a comparison of Burke and Kant, see Benjamin Delannoy, *Burke et Kant: interprètes de la revolution Française* (Paris: L'Harmattan, 2004).

[49] In particular Losurdo, *Immanuel Kant: Freiheit, Recht und Revolution*; Maus, *Zur Aufklärung der Demokratietheorie*; Kersting, *Wohlgeordnete Freiheit*.

[50] Achenwall, 'Iuris naturalis pars posterior', §§ 98, 101, 149. Christian Wolff, *Grundsätze des Natur – und Völkerrechts worin alle Verbindlichkeiten und alle Rechte aus der Natur des*

the king commits to rule in the people's interest, and the people commit to not rebel against him.[51] But the people are released from their obligation if the king breaches the contract, and may rebel. Kant, like Rousseau, rejected the contract of subjection,[52] whose central flaw Kant takes to be the lack of any separate entity to adjudicate and enforce the contractual commitments between people and ruler. One party to a contract cannot unilaterally withdraw, and third-party arbitration leads to infinite regress. A people cannot be both a party to the contract *and* its judge:

> In an already existing civil constitution, the people's judgment to determine how the constitution should be administered is no longer valid. For suppose that the people can so judge, and indeed judge contrary to the judgment of the actual head of state; who is to decide on which side the right is? Neither can make the decision as judge in its own suit. Hence there would have to be another head above the head of state, that would decide between him and the people; and this is self-contradictory. [...] Only he who possesses the supreme administration of public right can [decide the issue], and that is precisely the head of state; and no one in the commonwealth can, accordingly, have a right to contest his possession of it. (TP 8: 300, cf. Refl 19: 575)

Hobbes had already made a similar argument.[53] Although Kant's alignment with a theorist who championed unaccountable government is puzzling, scholars tend to agree that he was actually defending the supremacy of law.[54] The legal system, which has the final say as the voice of the community, replaces the many substantive disagreements that arise in societies.[55] If the legal system's authority can also be overruled, there is no conclusive way to establish justice.[56] Those who wish to change the law itself must do so through established procedures.

Menschen in einem beständigen Zusammenhange hergeleitet werden, Zweyte und verbesserte Auflage (Halle: in der Rengerischen Buchhandlung, 1769), p. 709.

[51] Wolff, *Grundsätze des Natur- und Völkerrechts*, pp. 694, 709; Wolff, *Deutsche Politik. Vernünftige Gedanken von dem gesellschaftlichen Leben der Menschen und und insonderheit dem gemeinen Wesen*, edited by Hasso Hoffmann (Munich: Verlag C. H. Beck, 2004), p. 180.

[52] Rousseau wrote, 'There is only one contract in the state, that of association, and that alone excludes any other'. *Social Contract*, 3.16. Cf. Kant Refl 19: 593. See also Maus, *Zur Aufklärung der Demokratietheorie*, p. 43ff; Kersting, *Wohlgeordnete Freiheit*, p. 457ff.

[53] A legal right of resistance triggers infinite regress: 'it setteth the Lawes above the Soveraign, setteth also a Judge above him, and a Power to punish him; which is to make a new Soveraign; and again for the same reason a third, to punish the second; and so continually without end, to the Confusion and Dissolution of the Common-Wealth'. See Thomas Hobbes, *Leviathan*, edited by Richard Tuck (Cambridge: Cambridge University Press, 1996), p. 224.

[54] Ripstein, *Force and Freedom*, p. 330.

[55] Jeremy Waldron, 'Kant's Theory of the State', in *Kant: Toward Perpetual Peace and Other Writings on Politics, Peace, and History*, edited by Pauline Kleingeld (New Haven: Yale University Press, 2006), pp. 179–200.

[56] Thomas Pogge, 'Kant's Theory of Justice', in *Kant-Studien* 79 (1988): 407–33.

Kant's rejection of a legal right of resistance probably originated in the doctrine of royal inviolability (sovereign immunity), the Roman law rule that holds that a head of state can do no legal wrong (*rex non potest peccare*) and cannot be prosecuted or punished.[57] Since only the monarch can punish, no one else can punish him. This was a standard element of the doctrine of sovereign immunity, which Hobbes also referenced, and which Kant refers to as English practice (MM 6: 317).[58] In his reflections on the philosophy of law from the 1770s, Kant very often mentioned the notion that the sovereign can do no wrong because no coercive rights can be enforced against him (Refl 7713, 7756, 7818, 7852). The claim has two steps: first, the sovereign defines the public view of right and wrong for the community through public law according to the standard of the original contract (TP 8: 294; Refl 19: 572). Second, the executive power must be legally unopposable (*irresistibel*) since several entities with coercive rights cannot coexist, and it would be 'self-contradictory' for the ruler – who cannot coerce itself – to be subject to coercion (TP 8: 299; MM 6: 317). However, Kant's legalistic argument against a right of resistance cannot in itself exclude all justified resistance, because rebels can also appeal to natural law or the sovereignty of the people, rather than breach of contract. Such defences of resistance and revolution raise other issues, though. Those resisting public legal authority could never be justified in claiming that they acted from an impartial and universal perspective because the people can only act through the constitutional order, mediated by its representatives, meaning that the people cannot act against that very same authority:

> For, since a people must be regarded as already united under a general legislative will in order to judge with rightful force about the supreme authority (*summum imperium*), it cannot and may not judge otherwise than the present head of state (*summum imperans*) wills it to. (MM 6: 318)

Only an omnilateral perspective, aligned with the idea of an original contract representing the general will of the people, can justify the use of force for the sake of right. That perspective, however, implies the existence of a set of legislative, executive, and judicial procedures that exist only in a civil condition. The sovereign, who holds legislative authority, can justifiably claim to speak on behalf of the people, because its task is to represent their united wills. A people acting against its representative can only act *per turbas*, as a mob (Refl 19: 591). Although from a moral perspective the sovereign can err

---

[57] Janelle Greenberg, 'Our Grand Maxim of State, "The King Can Do No Wrong"', in *History of Political Thought* 12, no. 2 (1991).

[58] 'Hurt inflicted on the representative of the commonwealth is not Punishment, but an act of Hostility: Because it is of the nature of Punishment, to be inflicted by publique Authority, which is the Authority only of the Representative it self'. Hobbes, *Leviathan*, p. 216.

substantively, no moral challenge to these established procedures by a group claiming to represent the people has coercive rights against the ruler. As Korsgaard has pointed out, well-intentioned rebels always act paternalistically, seizing the people's institutions for the sake of an essentially private view of the good.[59] Revolution returns civil society to the state of nature, contradicting the postulate of public right, which stipulates that those who unavoidably interact must submit to public legal authority so everyone can enjoy equal freedom under law. Regimes produced by successful revolutions must be obeyed, their illegitimate origins notwithstanding (MM 6: 323; TPP 8: 373). Their juridical status makes returning society to anarchy impermissible and removes the option of counter-revolution.[60]

3 Reform: 1789

In *The Metaphysics of Morals*, Kant claimed that, since Louis XVI had abdicated in the spring of 1789, the transfer of power from the monarch to the people was a legal reform rather than a revolution. He called the abdication an 'error of judgment'. King Louis had convened the Estates General to consult them on fiscal matters, but in convoking them, and in granting the unified assembly the right to decide on a limited topic (taxes), sovereignty was transferred to the assembly. Kant believed that Louis XVI had mistakenly assumed that sovereignty was divisible and could be loaned out like private property. What happened instead was that Louis XVI's sovereign authority vanished in its entirety and was transferred the new National Assembly. This rendered the central event of the revolution a *metamorphosis*, not a *palingenesis* – a change of the existing order, not its death and subsequent rebirth as an entirely new order. The metamorphosis had resulted in a new status quo wherein the nation exercised its constituent power: it was not the result of coercive action against the monarch, nor had society reverted to the state of nature. The commoners had not enforced moral principles against legal procedures; they had simply seized the opportunity offered them by the head of the state. Kant's interpretation justified the spring 1789 events in Versailles and protected the revolution against Bourbon dynasty legitimist claims. He was not contradicting his own

---

[59] Korsgaard, 'Taking the Law into Our Own Hands'.

[60] Domenico Losurdo has argued that Kant's rejection of resistance should be seen as strategic, and an argument against the French counter-revolution. Kant's argument would have condemned the 1793 Catholic uprisings in the Vendée. See *Immanuel Kant: Freiheit, Recht und Revolution*, p. 34. The problem with Losurdo's interpretation is that Kant's argument against resistance is independent of his views of the aims of the revolutionaries. As an argument about sovereignty, it holds across the board, against absolutist monarchy, republicanism, and so on.

injunction against the justice of revolution because he did not consider it a revolution.

Scholars have called Kant's argument an 'ingenious rationalization',[61] casuistry, sophistry,[62] legerdemain,[63] and an attempt to justify the revolution ex post facto.[64] These commentators have speculated that this was Kant's way, in the words of Dieter Henrich, of 'uniting his head with his heart'.[65] Although the revolution's liberal ideals had captured his heart, his head concluded that violence against the monarch could not be used to realise those ideals. He solved the dilemma by casuistically concluding that the event was not a revolution. Successfully defending this claim entails denying that the transfer of power was violent and arguing that a king could accidentally abandon sovereignty. As Peter Burg notes, Kant declines to explain why the monarch's intention to retain sovereignty was irrelevant.[66] Nor does he explain why that abdication did not return the people to the state of nature but constituted them as a legal entity.

Scholars who have tried to answer those questions have come up with a more sympathetic interpretation of Kant's argument. Domenico Losurdo and Ingeborg Maus have sought to show that it follows from his commitment to popular sovereignty. In fact, the situation in France in 1789 cannot be described as 'rebellion', wherein a faction of the people claiming to represent the whole takes the law in their own hands and seizes power.[67] This is because Louis XVI at Versailles organised the unified people through the Estates General and gave it the authority to decide. The people were no longer under the monarch's authority, because it had not contracted away its original right, simply delegated it to its representative. This made the transfer of power legal, so not a revolution, which Kant defined as a rebellion that returns society to the state of nature.[68] That claim also raises issues, however. Importantly, Louis XVI did not convene the people as a nation but as a fragment of the ancient estates. The Third Estate

---

[61] Harry van der Linden, *Kantian Ethics and Socialism* (Indianapolis, IN: Hackett Publishing Company, 1988), p. 178.

[62] Howard Williams, *Kant's Political Philosophy* (Oxford: Basil Blackwell, 1983), p. 212.

[63] Genevieve Rousseliere, 'On Political Responsibility in Post-revolutionary Times: Kant and Constant's Debate on Lying', in *European Journal of Political Theory* 17, no. 2 (2018): 227.

[64] Frederick Rauscher, 'Did Kant Justify the French Revolution Ex Post Facto?', in Robert R. Clewis (ed.), *Reading Kant's Lectures* (Berlin, Boston: De Gruyter, 2015), pp. 325–45.

[65] Henrich, 'On the Meaning of Rational Action in the State', p. 111.

[66] Burg, *Kant und die Französische Revolution*, p. 210.

[67] Losurdo, *Immanuel Kant: Freiheit, Recht und Revolution*, pp. 66–7; Maus, *Zur Aufklärung der Demokratietheorie*, p. 75.

[68] We should also note that Kant elsewhere had refrained from calling the events of 1789 a revolution. *Critique of the Power of Judgment* describes the events of 1789 as a 'fundamental transformation' (5: 375).

simply demanded recognition as the representative of the nation and threatened to use force to reach its goal.

Both Kant's critics and supporters must address the issue of popular violence in the transition. Although the transition was violent – after all, it was the French Revolution – Kant's account focuses on just one specific, very crucial event, not the entire sequence that followed it. Since there was no shortage of violent revolutionary events in the years that followed, including the fall of the constitutional monarchy, the declaration of the republic in 1792, and subsequent regicide (which, as we shall see in the next section, Kant designated as 'revolutionary') our perception of the 1788–9 events can easily be coloured by the ensuing drama. But the scope of Kant's argument was narrower, and to prove him wrong one must argue convincingly either that the king's abdication did not transfer sovereignty in 1789, or that he was forced to abdicate.

Harry van der Linden and Howard Williams have pursued the latter approach. As van Linden correctly notes, the commoners invoked no legal foundation for their claims. Appealing neither to established law nor to the monarch's will, they simply claimed to be the authentic representatives of the nation.[69] Williams argues that the claim succeeded because it was backed by the threat of violence. 'The truth of the matter was that he [Louis XVI] was forced to give up his absolute authority by the violent events going around him'.[70] Thus, the claim is that the agents lacked legal standing and used violence to pursue their ends. Yet, Kant's text is ambiguous, and it is unclear which event he has in mind: was it the convocation of the Estates General in May 1789 (an act that likely meets some threshold of voluntariness on the part of the king, yet which was clearly not an abdication), or was it the king's assent to the demands of the self-constituted National Assembly and the subsequent tennis court oath (clearly an abdication, but hardly voluntary). Or was it some third event – or the entire sequence of events that spring? Furthermore, if the king's abdication was not coerced, how could he, an absolute monarch, have abdicated accidentally? Any satisfactory answer to these questions calls for a more careful parsing of Kant's argument and the contextual evidence.

3.1 Kant's History of 1789

I now briefly present Kant's account of Louis XVI's accidental abdication and explore some challenging aspects of this account in historical context. As Kant's critics are quick to point out, by putting responsibility squarely on the king's shoulders, Kant seems to justify the 1789 revolution. Indeed, although his

---

[69] van der Linden, *Kantian Ethics and Socialism*, p. 178.
[70] Howard Williams, *Kant's Political Philosophy*, p. 212.

account raises some issues, it is a plausible interpretation given Kant's premise, presented in the first section of this essay, that supreme authority is originally in the people, which the king merely represented (MM 6: 341). Kant situates his brief account of the 1789 events at Versailles in the 1797 *Metaphysics of Morals*. He assumes that King Louis XVI's regime was despotic (as opposed to a republican form of government) since it combined legislative and executive powers in one entity. Nevertheless, as a state with laws, courts, and a sovereign, which had removed people from the state of nature, it was legitimate, the monarch had a right to rule, and the subjects had a duty to obey. An autocrat, Louis embodied the idea of the head of state, the unity of the commonwealth. Kant indents his text to emphasise that it is an application of his basic principles:

> A powerful ruler in our time therefore made a very serious error in judgment when, to extricate himself from the embarrassment of large state debts, he left it to the people to take this burden on itself and distribute it as it saw fit [*daß er es dem Volk übertrug, diese Last nach dessen eigenem Gutbefinden selbst zu übernehmen und zu vertheilen*]; for then the legislative authority naturally came into the people's hands, not only with regard to the taxation of subjects but also with regard to the government [*Regierung*], namely to prevent it from incurring new debts by extravagance or war. The consequence was that the monarch's sovereignty [*Herrschergewalt*] wholly disappeared (it was not merely suspended) and passed to the people, to whose legislative will the belongings of every subject became subjected. (MM 6: 341)

Kant says the people assumed both the debt and the authority to decide on how to pay it. By authorising the transfer, whether or not he intended it as a temporary delegation rather than a permanent transfer of authority, Louis XVI explicitly conceded that the National Assembly was the highest authority. The monarch intended it to be just a temporary delegation and not a permanent transfer of authority. After all, he had just authorised it to legislate on a single topic (finance) for a short period (to stave off the crisis), as a sort of agreement with the Estates General. Yet Kant denies that the new assembly could be legally bound by any agreement with the monarch:

> Nor can it be said that in this case one must assume a tacit but still contractual promise of the National Assembly [*Nationalversammlung*] not to make itself the sovereign [*zur Souveränität zu constituiren*] but only to administer this business of the sovereign and, having attended to it, return the reins of government into the monarch's hands; for such a contract is in itself null and void. The right of supreme legislation in a commonwealth is not an alienable right but the most personal of all rights [*das allerpersönlichste Recht*]. Whoever has it can control the people only through the collective will of the people; he cannot control the collective will itself, which is the ultimate basis of any public contract. A contract that would impose obligation on the

people to give back its authority would not be incumbent upon the people as the legislative power, yet would still be binding upon it; and this is a contradiction, in accordance with the saying 'No one can serve two masters.' (MM 6: 341)

It was not a mere temporary delegation of authority to the National Assembly, because the assembly was made sovereign. A sovereign could not be contractually bound to return power to a former sovereign after a designated term, because as sovereign it is the *source* of all juridically binding expressions of right and wrong and can abrogate any contract at will. Any higher court that could uphold the validity of such a contract would *itself* be sovereign. The idea of the general will is the only limit on the sovereign (just as the law of nature is the only limit on Hobbes's sovereign). This was Louis XVI's error: he mistakenly believed he could temporarily alienate the office of representation, but once he delegated it to the people it was lost.

Kant's text describes the spring 1789 events and assesses their legal consequences. With regard to questions of fact, his central claim is that Louis XVI conferred the right to decide on how to discharge the national debt, which entailed both exercising their authority to levy taxes and run the government, on the people. Although this is arguably true, the reality is more complicated. It is true that Louis XVI set the process in motion on 8 August 1788, by convoking an assembly for 5 May 1789 (and that he did so in order to solve a dire economic situation), but that was not the National Assembly, but the Estates General. The Estates General was as an essentially feudal assembly consisting of the clergy, the nobility, and the commoners – the Third Estate. These constituted the mixed government of the late medieval order that predominated before absolutism. It had not met since 1614. It is also true that, although he was under significant duress, the king was responsible for the convocation. Louis XVI had not wanted to convene the Estates General; he did so because the *parlement* of Paris wanted to make government more accountable. That is why they blocked the revenue-raising tax reforms that would have released the monarch from huge debts. The members of the *parlement* became popular heroes for standing up to absolutism, and although some unrest followed, the *parlement*'s demand for an Estates General was not illegal, but authorised by the 1614 precedent. Rather than respond with further repression, the king took his finance minister's suggestion and agreed to revive the ancient institution. He did not ask the assembly to make *decisions*, however. The king's convocation April 1789 letter merely requested his loyal subjects' counsel and assistance (*nous conceiller & nous assister*).[71]

---

[71] Louis XVI, 'Lettre du Roi pour la convocation des états-généreux', À Versailles, le 27 Avril 1789, Paris, De l'imprimerie royale, p. 3.

Although the result was not what the king actually wanted, the process did not amount to an insurrection (*Meuterei*) in Kant's sense, since it was an act by public officials and not a violent mob, and contradicted no law.

Yet, Kant does not say that the king convened the Estates General (a name he does not mention), but that he left the decision on taxation to the *National Assembly* (*Nationalversammlung*). The National Assembly came into being on 17 June, after the Third Estate led by Sieyès demanded that all the three estates be combined into one assembly that represented the nation. The result empowered the commoners, who had more deputies and could outvote the nobility and clergy. Although Louis XVI initially tried to reject this demand because it would cost him support, the assembly was determined to draft a new constitution. On 27 June he relented and ordered the remaining nobles and clergy to join the National Assembly. One of Kant's reflections shows he considered this to be decisive event: 'Thus the estates forming a coalition was just what raised a power against the king' (Refl 19: 595).[72]

The difference between the Estates General and the National Assembly was significant: the former represented the regions and estates, whereas the latter represented the nation. Sieyès justified this innovation with the principle of equal freedom, which originated with Rousseau. Only the principle of popular sovereignty could simultaneously secure individual freedom and public authority, a government accountable to the people. So the instant it was established, the National Assembly inherited the king's sovereignty and represented the united general will. It seems reasonable to assume that this explains Kant's comment that the monarch was letting 'the people' decide, since the assembly's legitimacy was grounded in its claim to represent the nation. It is unlikely that Kant construed the king's convocation of the Estates General as the 'mistake' – the instance when he abrogated sovereign authority.[73]

---

[72] Translation slightly amended.

[73] Could it be the case, rather, that Kant was actually thinking of the king's convocation of the Estates General, but that since he considered its purpose to be to represent the nation, that it was *equivalent* to the National Assembly? In German, *Nationalversammlung* can be both a proper name and a generic noun, and so use of that name does not necessarily indicate that he was thinking of the specific institution that did not come into being until 17 June, 1789. Yet for this interpretation to make sense, Kant must have either overlooked the fact that the Estates General represented the orders and regions (which seems implausible given his knowledge of the events), or he must have *denied* the legitimacy of the late feudal assembly. He did not do that though, but stated that such institutions could be 'provisionally' valid until the 'true republic' was instituted (MM 6: 340). This distinguished Kant from Sieyès, who refused to recognise the legitimacy of the orders of the late feudal estate society, and simply used the term National Assembly as equivalent to the Estates General. See Emmanuel Joseph Sieyès, 'Views of the Executive Means Available to the Representatives of France', in *Political Writings: Including the Debate between Sieyès and Tom Paine in 1791*, edited by Michael Sonenscher (Indianapolis, IN: Hackett Publishing Company, 2003), pp. 1–67.

Did the Third Estate's unilateral demand for recognition as a National Assembly meet Kant's threshold for revolution? It was an act of disobedience against the king and lacked legal foundation. The Third Estate had barricaded itself in the tennis court at Versailles and vowed to stay in session until the king agreed to their demand to be the sovereign representative of the French Nation. It was also a unilateral attempt to seize the authority that had belonged to the other two estates, and a breach of the trust of the voters who had sent the deputies to the Estates General to represent their interests, not the national interest.[74] Kant does not seem to think so, however. He writes that Louis XVI 'let himself' be represented and 'left it' to the people, meaning the monarch made an explicit choice.

This might appear to be a revisionist history that would serve the interest of the 1789 liberals (who had regained power by the time Kant wrote *The Metaphysics of Morals*). Yet I want to suggest that Kant was specifically commenting on Louis XVI's *Séance Royale* of 23 June, where the monarch allowed the three estates to deliberate together on a limited topic (taxation) and for a limited time (one session).[75] The *Séance Royale* was a momentous event whose reports Kant probably read, and whose content aligns with Kant's analysis of the king's mistaken belief that sovereignty could be temporarily alienated and limited in scope. The king's speech to the estates begins by rejecting the Third Estate's demand for recognition as the National Assembly, declaring it 'null' (*nulle*).[76] But then he allows them to meet as a single chamber just *once*, a compromise encouraged by his finance minister, Jacques Necker, who was seeking to pacify the defiant commoners. Necker had earlier convinced the king to double the membership of the Third Estate, which had no practical effect so long as voting was by order and not individual. In the *Séance* Louis XVI also discussed the matter of sovereignty, the right to decide. He admitted that, although the assembly had to consent to public debt, which could

---

[74] The delegates of the Estates General were subject to a binding mandate from their voters, and in conflicts between the national and the local interest were under a legally enforceable obligation to represent their orders, not the nation. See Louis XVI, 'Regulations for the Convocation of the Estates General (January 24 1789)' in *The Old Regime and the French Revolution*, edited by John W. Boyer and Julius Kirshner (Chicago and London: The University of Chicago Press, 1987), pp. 180–4, p. 182.

[75] Louis XVI allowed the estates 'to unite themselves during this session of estates only, to deliberate in common upon the affairs of general utility'. The king specifically denied their right to discuss the nature of the constitution and government. See 'Declaration of the King upon the States-General. June 23, 1789', in Frank Maloy Anderson, *The Constitutions and Other Select Documents Illustrative of the History of France, 1789–1901* (Minneapolis, MN: H. W. Wilson Company, 1904), p. 4.

[76] Louis XVI, 'Declaration of the King', p. 4; 'Discours du Roi lors de la séance royale du 23 juin 1789', *Archives Parlementaires de 1787 à 1860 – Première série (1787–1799) Tome VIII – Du 5 mai 1789 au 15 septembre 1789* (Paris: Librairie Administrative P. Dupont, 1875), p. 143.

lead to higher taxes,[77] he *still* had veto power over any and all proposals.[78] This was more than just a shift from his April 1789 convocation letter, which merely asked for counsel and assistance; it was actually a division and alienation of sovereignty.

First, it divided the scope of supreme authority, separating taxation from other government functions. Kant explicitly denied the validity of this distinction, first because the topics are inherently intertwined and could precipitate conflicts between an assembly and a monarch if both claim the right to decide, and second because it implied that sovereignty could be temporarily alienated. Louis XVI gave the assembly the right to decide *and* reserved the right to veto. In other words, the monarch granted the assembly sovereign decision-making power while reserving the right to withdraw it at any time.[79] It is puzzling that Kant does not mention the king's veto, which one might think would secure that his authority was not transferred to the assembly. Louis XVI's claim of veto power amounted to the claim that he had *not* given up sovereign authority, yet in Kant's view the people had the original supreme authority, and once the king assembled the people he could no longer claim to be their supreme representer. Kant therefore denied that a people can be bound to 'give back its authority' to a former sovereign, writing that any such agreement would be 'null and void' (*null und nichtig*, MM 6: 341). Kant's choice of words is significant, since Louis XVI had started the *Séance Royale* by declaring 'null' the Third Estate's claim to be the National Assembly. This linguistic trace strengthens the argument that Kant's text was a response to that momentous speech. Louis XVI's sad mistake was to misapprehend two key aspects of sovereignty: that its scope is unlimited

---

[77] 'As the borrowing of money might lead to an increase of taxes, no money shall be borrowed without the consent of the Estates-General', Louis XVI, 'Declaration of the King', p. 5.

[78] 'Reflect, gentlemen, that none of your dispositions can have the force of a law without my special approbation.' Louis XVI, 'Declaration of the King', p. 10.

[79] Louis XVI's compromise was likely an attempt to square his supposedly absolute power with the inescapable demands of the Estates General. This recalled the roles of the Estates General and the monarch during the late feudal era, which Otto Gierke called a dualistic regime. The estates and the monarch were co-authorities, and the monarch would need their consent to establish taxes and administer the territory in what remained largely subsistence economies. Absolutism had ended that system, but Louis XVI's desperate financial situation in 1789 led him to bring it back because he was powerless to impose taxes without the consent of the estates. As Jon Elster notes, even absolutist monarchs needed constant loans for their wars, and were therefore somewhat dependent. See Gierke, *Natural Law and the Theory of Society 1500 to 1800*, translated by Ernest Barker (Boston, MA: Beacon Press, 1957), p. 53ff; Catherine B. A. Behrens, *Society, Government, and the Enlightenment: The Experiences of Eighteenth Century France and Prussia* (London: Thames and Hudson, 1985), pp. 14–15; Charles Tilly, 'War Making and State Making as Organized Crime', in *Bringing the State Back In*, edited by Peter B. Evans, Dietrich Rueschemeyer, and Theda Skocpol (Cambridge: Cambridge University Press, 1985), pp. 169–91, p. 174; Kurt Wolzendorff, *Staatsrecht und Naturrecht* (Breslau: M & M Marcus, 1916), and Jon Elster, *France Before 1789: The Unraveling of an Absolutist Regime* (Princeton, NJ: Princeton University Press, 2020), p. 1.

and indivisible, and that it cannot be given away to the people and then taken back like property. We shall return to the philosophical ground for that claim shortly.

Although Kant's theory that Louis XVI was to blame for the rise of the commoners is usually seen as revisionist, it was shared by several conservatives, including Edmund Burke. Burke had initially welcomed the king's convocation of the Estates General as the end of absolutism and the return to the mixed government of the ancient constitution ('This constitution by estates, was the natural, and only just representation of France'[80]). But Louis XVI's decision, first to increase the Third Estate and then to permit the National Assembly, destroyed this option: 'With his own hand, however, Louis the Sixteenth pulled down the pillars which upheld his throne.'[81] In a note to his translation of Burke, Friedrich Gentz added that Necker 'was the true founder of the revolution'.[82] Thus, like Kant, Burke and Gentz attributed the causes of the revolution to the king and his advisors. 'These changes unquestionably, the King had no right to make', Burke wrote, and they were the root cause of the country 'perishing'.[83] He also blamed the representatives of the Third Estate of course, but in seizing power they had merely 'availed themselves of circumstances',[84] the chief circumstance being, of course, the king's reckless change to the traditional order of the estates. Gentz, Kant's former student and assistant in 1790, may well have conveyed this view to Kant.[85]

As this overview shows, Kant had a fairly good grasp of the events, and as the examples of Burke and Gentz indicate, his view that Louis XVI was responsible for ending his own regime was relatively common, even among conservatives. But blaming the king for what happened is not the same as defending the

---

[80] Edmund Burke, 'Letter to a Member of the National Assembly', in *Reflections on the Revolution in France*, edited by L. G. Mitchell (Oxford: Oxford University Press, 1993), pp. 251–92, pp. 284 and 289.

[81] Edmund Burke, 'Thoughts on French Affairs, etc., etc., written in December, 1791', in *The Works of the Right Honorable Edmund Burke*, vol. 4 (Boston, MA: Little, Brown and Company, 1869), p. 362.

[82] Friedrich Gentz, *Betrachtungen über die französische Revolution: In Zwei Theilen. Nach dem Englischen des Herrn Burke neu-bearbeitet mit einer Einleitung, Anmerkungen, politischen Abhandlungen, und einem critischen Verzeichniß der in England über diese Revolution erschienenen Schriften* (Berlin: Vieweg, 1793), p. 58.

[83] Burke, 'Letter to a Member of the National Assembly', p. 285.

[84] Edmund Burke, *Reflections on the Revolution in France*, edited by L. G. Mitchell (Oxford: Oxford University Press, 1993), p. 165.

[85] A further objection might be Kant's claim that sovereignty fell in the hands of 'the people'. That might seem like a significant exaggeration, since the Third Estate came from the propertied class and were elected by property holders, while both women and ordinary workers were excluded. However, Kant probably thought the Third Estate was mandated to represent the people, and as bearers of the united general will of the people could, by a form of synecdoche, be considered 'the people'.

revolution's legitimacy. Kant's description of the monarch's abdication as an accident may be partially correct since the monarch was unable to foresee the consequences of his acts. Yet Kant glosses over the Third Estate's aggressive assertion of itself as the sovereign assembly. Although the monarch gave in to them, first a little by allowing them one joint session, and then entirely when that failed to appease them, he was under significant duress. It is not clear whether he had much of a choice, since he would probably have been removed by force if he refused to make concessions. Kant's analysis is primarily legal, however, tracing the king's accidental abdication to his failure to grasp the legal consequences of setting up a new representative assembly.

3.2 Defending the National Assembly's Sovereignty

Kant's account of the historical events surrounding Louis XVI's delegation of authority to the Estates General, and his subsequent loss of sovereignty, has some plausibility. Establishing the truth of the claim, however, entails context-ualising the historical reality in a frame of legal and political principles. We shall now scrutinise how Kant applied his juridical principles of sovereignty to the case of revolutionary France. We should expect to find selective applications of the theory if Kant, as scholars have claimed, was looking to justify his sympathy for the revolution. Yet, as I will argue, Kant's conclusions were supported both by his own legal and political principles, and by the guiding principles of French absolutism.

As we saw in the previous section, Kant's basic view is that the sovereign, which embodies the ideal of the head of state, represents the united will of the people. The right to rule is neither private property predicated on a particular bloodline or history, nor a contractual relation between the people and sover-eign, as Achenwall had maintained.[86] Rather, sovereignty comes from the very status inhering in the nation's representative (*Stellvertreter*) endowed with legislative authority and power to enforce the law. Louis XVI erred on two counts: that sovereignty could be divided (that the National Assembly repre-sented the people on taxation) and that it could be temporarily alienated (that the National Assembly could be contractually bound to return it). Kant argued that by inviting the National Assembly to represent the people, it took on supreme legislative power and thereby he abdicated his sovereignty. He presents this view in paragraph 51 of *The Metaphysics of Morals*, which discusses

---

[86] Because the sovereign, in Achenwall's view, depended on a contractual relation between people and ruler, neither party to the contract may unilaterally breach it: the monarch may not abdicate without consent, nor can the people abdicate him. See *Iuris naturalis pars posterior* §. 155.

a sovereign who establishes a separate assembly. This must be Louis XVI since it immediately precedes application of the argument to France:

> But as soon as a person who is head of state (whether it be a king, nobility, or the whole of the population, the democratic union) also lets itself be represented, then the united people does not merely *represent* the sovereign: it is the sovereign itself. For in it (the people) is originally found the supreme authority from which all rights of individuals as mere subjects (and in any event as officials of the state) must be derived. (6: 341)

There are two steps to this argument: first, the sovereign appoints a representative assembly to legislate in the name of the general united will of the commonwealth. This delegation, Kant claims, was equivalent to giving that assembly supreme decision-making power (i.e. sovereignty), which is always a property of the entity that legally embodies the unity of the commonwealth. Second, in so doing, the monarch is accepting representation as a private individual (a part of the general united will), *not* as a sovereign, since sovereignty has been transferred to the new assembly. That new assembly does not just represent the sovereign monarch, it *is* sovereign. The idea of the people as the original supreme authority is a reference to the original contract, which establishes the basic principle of popular sovereignty.[87] The monarch's power had only been derived from the people, and when the people was present as a legally constituted entity, it naturally assumed authority.

This does not mean that a monarch risks losing sovereignty every time he appoints an advisory council, such as a privy council. The National Assembly was not merely a committee, but the unified people whose will the king merely had represented. Once Louis XVI abandoned his legislative authority to the united people, he ceased to represent the united will and the new assembly instead represented it, since the sovereign's authority had been suspended. Kant noted that: 'if even once he calls them [the people] together and constitutes them as such, then not only is his authority suspended but it can also be broken off entirely, like the standing of every representative when the one who gave him that power is himself present' (Refl 19: 593). For this reason, the king's claim to retain the right to veto was without force. Louis XVI had merely represented the

---

[87] Maus has called attention to this, but she has argued that Kant's talk of the united people being the sovereign shows that he had direct democracy in mind, and this need not be the case. 'The people' is sovereign only in the juridical sense that legislation is in the *name* of the people, which is compatible with a representative assembly. Karlfriedrich Herb and Bernd Ludwig have convincingly argued against Maus's claim by recalling the fact that Kant clearly had a representative assembly in mind when he wrote about the people in the above quote. See Maus, *Zur Aufklärung der Demokratietheorie*, p. 199, and Herb and Ludwig, 'Kants kritisches Staatsrecht', in *Jahrbuch für Recht und Ethik/Annual Review of Law and Ethics* 2 (1994): 466.

people, and once it was gathered and poised to legislate, he no longer represented it and his desire to have the final say had no authority.

But why could not sovereignty be delegated for specific purposes (such as taxation) and for a limited time? Kant claimed that Louis XVI's strategy of delegating supreme authority only on the issue of taxation backfired because the power to tax entails control of other authoritative governmental functions, such as the power to wage war. This argument is deeply rooted in Kant's theory of sovereignty, which claims that the sovereign has the authority of the supreme proprietor (*dominus territorii*), the public possessor (MM 6: 323). That implies 'the right to assign to each what is his', that is, to decide on property rights. Property rights secure mutual freedom only when they are established by a system of public law, hence the supreme proprietor is ultimately the legislator. Its authority over fiscal policy justified the sovereign's abolition of the property rights of the nobility and the Church, measures that echoed decisions of the French National Constituent Assembly.[88]

So when Louis XVI renounced the right to decide on fiscal policy, he abdicated the central task of sovereignty. Kant reveals this in a preliminary reflection:

> The national assembly was called in order to save the state by covering with their guarantee all the debts imposed upon the state by the extravagance of the regime (not merely to make plans). Thus they had to voluntarily guarantee [*verbürgen*] it with their property [added: they must therefore have put themselves in a condition where they alone could dispose of their property, hence in the condition of freedom under laws but such laws as they themselves would give, i.e. a republican or free civil condition] and the court [*der Hof*] had itself yielded the right to encumber them. But so that they could achieve this state of citizenry, they had to establish a constitution that could exercise no acts of authority over them. (Refl 19: 595)

If the National Assembly was to vouch for the national debt, it had to be the sole entity with power over private property. That was a condition of the people's freedom under the laws that they gave themselves, that is to say, a republican constitution. Here Kant relies on the argument from *Perpetual Peace*,

---

[88] A state can repeal the property rights of a 'knightly order' or a church 'if public opinion has ceased to favor military honors' or 'has ceased to want masses for souls'. 'Those affected by such reforms cannot complain of their property being taken from them, since the reason for their possession hitherto lay only in the people's opinion and also had to hold as long as that lasted' (MM 6: 324–5). On 4 August 1789, the National Constituent Assembly abolished the feudal system, including the seigneurial rights of the nobility and the tithes gathered by the Catholic clergy, and on 2 November it placed all church property 'at the disposition of the nation'. See Dale Van Kley, 'The Ancien Régime, Catholic Europe, and the Revolution's Religious Schism', in *A Companion to the French Revolution*, edited by Peter McPhee (Malden, MA: Wiley-Blackwell, 2012), pp. 123–44, p. 125.

mentioned in the previous section, which states that monarchs in republican constitutions need the consent of the citizens to declare war, since the citizens will bear the costs (TPP 8: 351). In republics, the citizens are distributively members of the state and collectively the state's supreme proprietor, and therefore subject to no higher authority. Louis XVI's request for the people's consent to raise taxes acknowledges that he lacked the right to tax them at will, since the united people, represented by their deputies, were actually the supreme proprietor. That recognition signalled a break with the absolutist system, which allowed monarchs to levy taxes without consent.[89] The result was Louis XVI's self-demotion to the merely executive function of constitutional monarch.

But why cannot sovereignty be temporarily alienated? In the *Séance Royale* Louis XVI had insisted that the delegation of sovereignty was merely temporary, and that the National Assembly had to return it once it had met. We shall now explore the legal foundation of Kant's claim that any such agreement would be null and void. The injunction relies on an earlier argument of Rousseau's, that sovereignty cannot be represented or temporarily alienated, since the entity representing or borrowing it would have supreme authority to decide on *everything*, including the scope, time limits, and validity of any and all contracts.[90] Temporary sovereignty was a contradiction, as it would render the people simultaneously sovereign (as legislator with the authority to decide on all contracts) and not sovereign (because it would be subjected to the contract).[91] This is why Kant notes: 'Thus if a king summons the people together through their representatives in order to reform the state, then no obligation prevents them from changing the state to an entirely different form, and they can take sovereignty upon themselves immediately' (Refl 19: 582). Once Louis XVI forfeited his role as sovereign, the people were no longer under direct obligation to him.[92]

---

[89] See for example Samuel Pufendorf, *On the Duty of Man and Citizen According to Natural Law*, edited by James Tully, translated by Michael Silverthorne (Cambridge: Cambridge University Press, 1991), p. 166.

[90] 'Sovereignty cannot be represented for the same reason that it cannot be alienated. It consists essentially in the general will, and the will does not allow of being represented. It is either itself or something else; there is nothing in between. The deputies of the people, therefore, neither are nor can be its representatives; they are merely its agents. They cannot conclude anything definitively.' Rousseau, *On the Social Contract*, 3.15.

[91] This does not imply that the sovereign assembly cannot establish laws limiting its power, and cannot make them difficult to change, but that it must remain the supreme authority on such laws.

[92] As mentioned in the previous section, the rejection of a contractual limit on sovereignty may also be a reference to the contract of subjection, where the people agree to be subject to the sovereign in return for protection. This had been standard in Wolffian natural law theory, which Kant rejected. Kant, like Hobbes, believed that no agreements formed prior to establishing the juridical condition could bind it, and contracts are binding only under the laws established by the sovereign. This has been argued by Losurdo, *Immanuel Kant: Freiheit, Recht und*

Kant, who considered sovereignty a matter of personal right, argued that conceiving it as something that could be temporarily alienated reduced it to a property right: 'The right of supreme legislation in a commonwealth is not an alienable right but the most personal of all rights [*das allerpersönlichste Recht*]' (MM 6: 341). By personal right, Kant means that it is not a right in a *thing* (which could be alienated) but a right vested in the *person* of the legislator. Kant's use of personal right (*ius personalissimum*) follows Achenwall,[93] and is based in the Roman law distinction between *Ius in personam*, a right vested in the individual that cannot be alienated, and *Ius in re*, which is a right to a specific property.[94] Personal rights include parental rights and the right of an author over his book (WUP 8:86; MM 6: 282). Although in Louis XVI's case a legal rather than a natural person had the right (he was the legislator), it remained a personal right, and the cases are analogous. Just as an author owns his words – has personal rights, or author's rights – the legislator owns – has personal rights over – his legislation. This does not reduce them to commodities: just as authors' rights (in Kant's view) cannot be bought and sold, sovereign rights cannot be temporarily loaned out or alienated. It might sound odd to say that sovereignty cannot be alienated *at all*, since Louis XVI in fact did alienate it in the sense that he ceased being sovereign. But Kant means that sovereignty cannot be treated like private property, which can be sold or leased at will, not that this precludes transfer from one entity or person to another. Treating sovereignty, or the state, like property implies setting a *private* will above the general will. So once it is transferred, sovereignty is lost. Violent seizures of power through revolution are more akin to murder than theft, because the revolutionary kills the political body, which is represented in the person of the embodied sovereign.

Kant's verdict on Louis XVI is therefore based on his own principles; he did not casuistically tailor the principles to justify his preferred outcomes. Nor were Kant's conclusions eccentric. They aligned with the official concept of sovereignty and the ideology of the French absolutism, which is why Kant described the king's action as an 'error of judgement' (*Fehltritt der Urtheilskraft*): it was not just wrong in terms of his philosophy, but in terms of the French tradition itself. Again, this might sound strange. French monarchs ruled by Salic law, which conferred hereditary kingship, and it had been customary in the previous couple of centuries to treat the king's will as absolute. That being the case, it

---

Revolution, p. 66; Kersting, *Wohlgeordnete Freiheit*; and Maus, *Zur Aufklärung der Demokratietheorie*, p. 75.
[93] Achenwall, 'Iuris naturalis pars posterior', § 159.
[94] Aaron X. Fellmeth and Maurice Horwitz, *Guide to Latin in International Law* (Oxford: Oxford University Press, 2009).

seems like the king's renunciation of power would have to be intentional; it could not simply slip out of his hands by mistake against his own expressed will.

Yet the French monarchy relied on a claim that resembled Kant's view of the sovereign as representative of the unity of the commonwealth. Jacques-Bénigne Bossuet, Louis XIV's court preacher and theologian, who provided the theoretical foundations of absolutism, defined the monarch as a public person who represented the unity of the commonwealth:

> The prince, as prince, is not regarded as a private person: he is a public personage, all the state is in him; the will of all the people is included in his [...] Behold an immense people united in a single person; behold this holy power, paternal and absolute; behold the secret cause which governs the whole body of the state, contained in a single head.[95]

Bodin, who is often credited as the founder of the modern concept of sovereignty, had already laid the groundwork for the idea in France. He defined sovereign authority as the supreme authority who delegated the authority to all other powers, and therefore could withdraw it: 'in his presence, all the power and jurisdiction of all magistrates, guilds and corporations, Estates and communities, cease'.[96] The sovereign monarch incorporated the unity of the commonwealth, a theory Bodin devised to undercut the claims to a right of resistance by intermediary power holders influenced by Huguenot resistance theory.[97] This is essentially the same idea that Skinner identified in Hobbes: the sovereign represents the person of the state (the *persona civitatis*), not the multitude of actual persons and estates.[98] Because sovereignty is unlimited, Hobbes refers to this as 'the absolute representative of all the subjects'.[99] That was why Louis XIV reputedly told the *parlement* that *l'état, c'est moi*: all of the king's public acts are automatically attributed to the person of the state. In the *Séance Royale* Louis XVI echoed that ideology when he addressed the Estates General, as 'their true representative' who had the last word. *Yet*, in the same speech, he admitted that the delegates were 'representing the nation' and had the right to decide. From Bossuet's and Kant's perspective this was an egregious error, since the commonwealth can have only one representative. The following reflection from a draft for *The Metaphysics of Morals* shows that Kant agreed with this basic feature of the theory of sovereignty:

---

[95] Jacques Bénigne Bossuet, *Political Treatise*, in *Readings in European History*, 2 vols., edited by James Harvey Robinson (Boston, MA: Ginn, 1906), p. 276.

[96] Jean Bodin, *On Sovereignty: Four Chapters from The Six Books of the Common Wealth*, edited and translated by Julian H. Franklin (Cambridge: Cambridge University Press, 1992), p. 115.

[97] Julian Franklin, *Jean Bodin and the Rise of Absolutist Theory* (New York: Cambridge University Press, 1973), p. 49.

[98] Skinner, 'Hobbes and the Purely Artificial Person', p. 21.   [99] Hobbes, *Leviathan*, p. 156.

> Thus the misfortune of the king comes directly from his own sovereignty, after he had once allowed all the people's deputies to assemble, then he was nothing; for his legislative power was founded only on his representing the whole people. (Refl 19: 595)

Kant's interpretation of the event can be read as an attempt to emphasise the fundamental premise of absolutism, which he shared with Hobbes and Bossuet. Thus, following both Kant and Bossuet, sovereignty *can* be lost unintentionally. It cannot be if the monarch's councillors unilaterally simply decide to take power, only if he confers on them the right to decide, abandoning his task of representing the unity of the people.[100]

Whether the sovereign was entitled to initiate this process is another matter. Earlier in paragraph 52, Kant had denied that sovereigns could change the state's constitution from autocracy to democracy, 'For even if the sovereign decided to transform itself into a democracy, it could still do the people a wrong, since the people itself could abhor such a constitution and find one of the other forms more to its advantage' (MM 6: 340). We might ask whether this is exactly what Louis XVI was doing, since he returned power to the nation's representatives. Yet that was not to create a new constitutional form, but to delegate the task to the nation's representatives. Achenwall had argued that when a monarch abandons sovereignty, power returns to the people, who can then decide what kind of constitution to establish.[101] Rousseau had supported a variation of this idea (without the contract of subjection), which became consequential in France in the spring of 1789 thanks to Sieyès's distinction between the *pouvoir constituant*, the power to constitute, and the *pouvoir constitué*, the constitutionally created authorities.[102] On the terms Sieyès established, the National Assembly was the *pouvoir constituant*, entitled to draft a new constitution – which is what it went on to do. By 9 July 1789 it had changed its name to National Constituent Assembly (*Assemblée nationale constituante*) and dissolved itself once the new

---

[100] Hobbes argued that sovereignty cannot be accidentally lost by 'error and misreckoning' of language. A sovereign granting a body of councillors the status of the absolute representative must 'plainly and directly discharge them of their subjection'. Yet this is in fact what Louis XVI did, when he *plainly and directly* stated that the representatives of the nation were to make decisions, even as he incoherently insisted on remaining the true representative. Hobbes, *Leviathan*, p. 156. In some striking passages Hobbes almost predicts what was to happen at Versailles in 1789, admonishing sovereigns that if they convoke an advisory body they must limit them either in time or 'by the nature of their business' (Hobbes, *Leviathan*, p. 162). Louis XVI tried to do just that, but that was little help since he had granted the assembly decision-making power.

[101] Achenwall, 'Iuris naturalis pars posterior', §§ 95, 159.

[102] As Thiele has argued, Kant was in agreement with Sieyès in this regard. See Repräsentation und Autonomieprinzip, p. 126. See also Herb and Ludwig, 'Kants kritisches Staatsrecht', p. 465.

constitution was established on 3 September 1791. So Louis XVI did not change the form of sovereignty, he left the decision up to the assembly. Although the assembly could have reinstated Louis XVI as the sovereign, they chose to set up a constitutional monarchy.

The king's de facto abdication raises the question of whether there was a brief moment of lawlessness before the National Assembly took power. The new sovereign could not have been *authorised* by the previous one, since its authority was only valid under the old regime. Kant never says that Louis XVI authorised the new assembly, simply that his sovereignty 'disappeared' and 'passed' to the people (MM 6: 341). Since Louis XVI could not have conferred power on the new sovereign, one might think there was a brief legal vacuum, in breach of the injunction of no reversion to the state of nature. Yet, the National Assembly was in session during the entire process, and there was no time in which a sovereign did not exist.[103]

Conceding that the king accidentally abandoned sovereignty does not entail agreeing that he renounced executive command of the coercive apparatus of the state. Does that create an interpretive challenge? After all, Kant considered superior coercive force a necessary (though not sufficient) part of sovereignty. Sovereignty must be both de jure and de facto. So if the new National Assembly did not control the armed forces, perhaps it was not sovereign at all. Yet once the National Assembly was constituted as the sovereign, the king became merely the chief executive in what was about to become a constitutional monarchy; as such, he acted on authority delegated by the National Assembly. Legally speaking, the National Assembly controlled the armed forces through the monarch. If the king decided to oppose the nation's delegates, *he* would be the rebel, and his acts would only challenge its power, while subtracting nothing from its authority. Whether the king had *independent* command over the forces is in this case a question of fact, concerning their obedience to him rather than the National Assembly. It was unclear in the spring of 1789 whether the armed forces were loyal to the king or whether their loyalty had been transferred to the new assembly. That question came to a head a little later in the summer of 1789, when the king's firing of Necker was widely seen as an attempt to claw back power. The king was forced to back down when the Bastille was stormed and only then did it become entirely clear that the National Assembly was fully in charge of the executive arm of government. In Kantian terms, Bastille Day could then be construed not as a rebellious act by the masses or the National Assembly, but as a counter-revolution by the king and the conservative factions supporting him.

---

[103] I am grateful to Sosuke Amitani for helpful discussions of this topic.

Not surprisingly, scholars have taken Kant's unusual interpretation with a grain of salt, mainly because it legitimises his preferred party, sounding just as ideological as the Whig version of the 1688 English Revolution, which portrayed an orderly and lawful transfer of sovereignty. Kant himself had criticised (and ridiculed) the Commons' and Lords' claims that King James had abdicated by breaking the original contract, saying they lacked the courage to call it a revolution.[104] But the situations are not analogous. In the French case there was no civil war or military force at the outset. There was little violence until the summer of 1789, when the transfer of sovereignty was already complete. Although the storming of the Bastille was a spectacular event, and critics of the theory of popular sovereignty like Edmund Burke seized on it to make the case against the new regime, it did not affect the juridical status of sovereignty. Louis XVI then formally accepted his role as a constitutional monarch and signed the 1791 constitution, which gave legal finality to the new regime.

If Kant's account of the events of 1789 is correct, it leads to the conclusion that an orderly, albeit accidental, reconstitution of the state as a republic took place, not a revolution. Kant was not, as Dieter Henrich maintained, trying to align his head with his heart, to solve the cognitive dissonance between his rejection of a right of revolution and his sympathy with the events in France. Besides, he had no systematic reasons for wanting to justify the origin of the new French regime. To be sure, he sympathised with the outcome of the transition, but for two reasons that would not require him to sympathise with the process. First, because it is perfectly possible to be pleased with a result without justifying the process.[105] Second, because Kant believed in the obligation to obey *any* existing government, regardless of its origins (MM 6: 371). Since the revolutionary government was a fact, it had to be obeyed, and there was no justification for counter-revolution. Kant genuinely believed the events in France did not amount to the kind of violent uprising he rejected on principled grounds.

Although the king initiated the transfer of sovereignty, which Kant believed was formally correct, the fact was that Louis XVI rejected the outcome. His public acceptance of the new regime notwithstanding, he secretly worked to instigate a counter-revolution with the help of *émigrés* and foreign monarchs. That cost him his head and led to a second revolution that put an end to constitutional monarchy once and for all. The next section discusses why Kant saw the rebellion against the constitutional monarch, and his execution, to be an unpardonable crime and a real revolution.

---

[104] Kant writes that the English Parliament did not want to admit the contractual right of revolution and therefore pretended that the monarch had abdicated voluntarily (TP 8: 299).

[105] Hill, 'Questions about Kant's Opposition to Revolution'.

4 Revolution: 1792

A long footnote in *The Metaphysics of Morals* argues that the rebellion and the trial of Louis XVI in the fall of 1792, followed by his execution in January 1793, were an attempt by the French to cloak a murder in a semblance of rightful procedure. Fear of the vengeance that might accompany a successful counter-revolution to reinstate the old regime drove the pretence of lawful punishment. Kant roundly condemned this strategy. A people can never judge its sovereign, who as the source of law can formally do no wrong (MM 6: 321). Once the people assume the role of judge over the sovereign, using force against the one who (formally) upholds the law, they overturn all concepts of right. When they dress such tactics up in legal procedure, it is 'as if the state commits suicide', because those claiming to protect the law are actually destroying its foundation, both in fact and principle. Instrumentalising the legal process for the purely political aim of securing power elevates politics above law. Upholding the people's right to judge its sovereign would 'make it impossible to generate again a state that has been overthrown' (MM 6: 322–3). Better to be honest and appeal to a right of necessity, which at least could have provided an *excuse* for the rebellion and regicide.

Kant described the rebellion, driven by the revolutionary Paris commune, which claimed to represent the French people, and the Jacobin faction in the legislative assembly, as an insurrection against both the monarch and the legitimate 1791 constitution. It suspended Louis XVI's authority and declared national elections for a new convention charged with drafting a republican constitution. Kant's condemnation of this was based on his prohibition against populist claims of a right of revolution, and expressed his support for the liberals who had established the National Assembly at Versailles in 1789. Kant's interpretation of the king's trial and execution aligns with historians who consider it an example of political justice.[106]

Shortly after publication of *The Metaphysics of Morals*, Johan Adam Bergk raised a fundamental objection: given that the 10 August revolution annulled the 1791 constitution and constituted the new National Convention as sovereign, at the time of his trial Louis XVI was an ordinary French citizen. Since the

---

[106] Jon Elster's four standards for political justice can be applied. First, there was no legal basis for the trial, since the constitution explicitly denied the right to prosecute the monarch, and the new National Convention held the king accountable to standards they invented as they went along. Second, there was no independent judiciary, since the legislature functioned as court, hence no professional judges. Third, the judges had a conflict of interest since the legislators owed their positions to the rebellion against the accused. Fourth, principles of due process were not respected: among other things law was applied retroactively, and there was no right to appeal or right to due deliberation. Jon Elster, *Closing the Books: Transitional Justice in Historical Perspective* (Cambridge: Cambridge University Press 2004), p. 79ff.

Convention addressed the former monarch as Louis Capet, the people were not sentencing their sovereign. Despite the fact that Kant considered the 10 August revolution unjust, he himself had pointed out that the legitimacy of the new regime could not be contested once a revolution has succeeded.[107] Karl Vorländer and Peter Burg have since made the same argument, with Burg adding that Kant was rewriting history so he could apply his own theory of the rejection of a right of resistance against a sovereign.[108] This is a serious objection, because punishing a *former* monarch seems to be less consequential than punishing a *reigning* monarch.

I will argue that Kant was defending the principle of sovereign immunity, which he considered to be valid for all sovereigns, present and former. Although the immediate consequences of punishing a reigning sovereign are more momentous than those following punishment of a former sovereign, Kant's concern is with the principle, not with the consequences in a specific time and place. The king's executioners sought to justify themselves by giving a desperate act of self-defence the veneer of legality. In so doing, they jettisoned the principle of sovereign immunity, attacking the very principle upholding all public authority and making it impossible to regenerate the state.

Could the principle of sovereign immunity be overturned for a good outcome? Michael Walzer has argued against Kant that the highly imperfect judicial procedures of the king's trial could be justified as a symbolic manifestation of the people as sovereign, thereby consolidating faith in the new republican regime: 'Revolutionary justice is defensible whenever it points the way to everyday justice.'[109] Formally *illegal* actions can be *legitimate* if they accord with a higher values. Ferenc Fehér has pushed back against Walzer, pointing out that the revolution failed on Walzer's own consequentialist criteria: the trial and execution of the king did not stabilise the new republic, since what followed was the terror, dissolution of political stability, and, after a generation, reinstitution of the monarchy.[110]

Kant opposed these types of consequentialist arguments about transitional justice. His concern is the very idea that the people can judge a (past or present) sovereign at all, a principle that he took to contradict the concept of public authority and to make it impossible to sustain the state. Kant did care about *that*

---

[107] Johann Adam Bergk, *Briefe über Immanuel Kant's Metaphysische Anfangsgründe der Rechtslehre, enthaltend Erläuterungen, Prüfung und Einwürfe* (Leipzig and Gera: bey Wilhelm Heinsius, 1797), p. 212.

[108] Vorländer, 'Kants Stellung zur Französischen Revolution', p. 260; Burg, *Kant und die Französische Revolution*, p. 211.

[109] Walzer, *Regicide and Revolution*, p. 79.

[110] Ferenc Fehér, 'Revolutionary Justice', in Michael Walzer, *Regicide and Revolution: Speeches at the Trial of Louis XVI* (New York: Columbia University Press, 1993), pp. 217–36, pp. 224–5.

consequence, which implied that the people would be forever trapped in the state of nature. This should come as no surprise to anyone familiar with Kant's argument against a right of revolution. His parallel argument about punishing a monarch is entirely based on the philosophical principle of sovereign inviolability. Kant held that it is always wrong to jettison law, and doing so amounts to building the new constitution on sand. Instrumentalising law for political ends amounts to identifying law entirely with strategic interests. In Kant's words, it 'would have to make it impossible to generate again a state that has been overthrown' (MM 6: 322). Although he was making a point about the injustice of a hypocritical attitude to law, the claim can easily be seen as an explanation of the events that followed the king's trial: a Jacobin coup, civil war, terror, and the implosion of the French state. Kant's verdicts on the 1789 and 1792 events were that the former represented popular action channelled through legitimate institutions, while the latter represented a unilateral claim to represent the people outside established law. As a result, the first French republic's foundation was tainted by politics disguised as justice.

4.1 Kant's History of 1792

Kant's account of the trial and execution of Louis XVI follows his discussion of the legal right to judge the sovereign, which we discussed in the first section. He argued that the people acting outside legal institutions had no such right, since that would allow them to judge their own case. No one has the right to judge the sovereign, because only the sovereign's verdict unifies the legal system and has the final say. The sovereign's verdict provides society with a shared view of justice, which allows citizens to judge right and wrong prospectively. Attacking the head of state is high treason, punishable by death 'for attempting to destroy his fatherland (*parricida*)' (MM 6: 319). Kant claims there are two ways to kill a king: assassination and formal execution.

> Of all the atrocities involved in overthrowing a state by rebellion, the *assassination* of the monarch is not itself the worst, for we can still think of the people as doing it from fear that if he remained alive he could marshal his forces and inflict on them the punishment they deserve, so that their killing him would not be an enactment of punitive justice but merely a dictate of self-preservation. It is the formal *execution* of a monarch that strikes horror in a soul filled with the idea of human rights, a horror that one feels repeatedly as soon as and as often as one thinks of such scenes as the fate of Charles I or Louis XVI. (MM 6: 320–1)

Although it is a crime, treason, to assassinate a king, the assassins can still appeal to the 'pretext' of a right of necessity [*Notrecht*] (*casus necessitatis*) for the sake of self-preservation. The principle of sovereign inviolability, however, condemns the people who would punish (present or past) sovereigns the way the French did:

> But it never has the least right to punish him, the head of state [*das Oberhaupt*], because of his previous administration, since everything he did, in his capacity as head of state, must be regarded as having been done in external conformity with rights, and he himself, as the source of the law, can do no wrong [*unrecht*]. (MM 6: 320–1; see also 314; TPP 8: 383)

Kant distinguishes between the maxims that motivate criminal murder and formal execution: although a criminal might make it his maxim to exempt himself from the valid principle of sovereign inviolability, in the French case the executioners made it their maxim to overturn *the principle itself.* That is a much worse transgression because, as we have seen, it attacks the very foundation of public authority. So the murder and execution of a sovereign are quite different things:

> The reason for horror at the thought of the formal execution of a monarch by his people is therefore this: that while his *murder* is regarded as only an *exception* to the rule that the people makes its maxim, his execution must be regarded as a complete *overturning* of the principles of the relation between a sovereign [*Souverän*] and his people (in which the people, which owes its existence only to the sovereign's legislation, makes itself his master), so that violence is elevated above the most sacred rights brazenly and in accordance with principle. Like a chasm that irretrievably swallows everything, the execution of a monarch seems to be a crime from which the people cannot be absolved, for it is as if the state commits suicide. (MM 6: 320)

Kant believed that the 1792 revolutionaries could not have been motivated to commit such a horrific crime. Rather, the formal execution of Louis XVI was a smokescreen to hide the fact that the murder was committed in self-defence:

> There is, accordingly, reason for assuming that the agreement to execute the monarch actually originates not from what is supposed to be a rightful principle but from fear of the state's vengeance upon the people if it revives at some future time, and that these formalities are undertaken only to give that deed the appearance of punishment, and so of a *rightful procedure* (such as murder would not be). But this disguising of the deed miscarries; such a presumption on the people's part is still worse than murder, since it involves a principle that would have to make it impossible to generate again a state that has been overthrown. (MM 6: 322)

Let us start by evaluating the facts of the matter, and in the next section probe Kant's analysis. First, we might wonder why Kant speaks of the French monarch as 'the sovereign'. After all, in the 1791 constitution, it was specified that the king rules only *by the law*, and that the National Assembly makes the law. That would make the legislature the sovereign. Yet, on Kantian grounds, the monarch could still be referred to as the sovereign, since Kant considered the true sovereign to be the (idea of the) head of state, which consisted of the three powers, with the legislature as the highest entity (the 'major premise' of a syllogism, as Kant said) and the king merely as executive. Thus, an act against the king would be an act against the sovereign legislature, and as such against the sovereign. One problem with this explanation is that Kant refers to the monarch as 'the source of law', meaning that he does not merely have the regent (*der Regent*) in mind, but the legislator (*der Beherrscher des Volks*). Probably, by 'source of law' Kant means something like the British idea of a 'king or queen in parliament', who must assent to legislation before it is promulgated. Indeed, that was the case with the French monarch: the 1791 constitution gave him a suspensive veto power over legislation. The fact that Louis XVI chose to hide in the parliament when his palace was under attack indicates just this awareness that his legitimacy as a constitutional monarch consisted in his position within a larger government structure.

There is another reason to wonder why Kant refers to Louis XVI as the sovereign at the time of the trial. As Bergk pointed out, when the proceedings started, Louis XVI was no longer the sovereign as the 10 August revolution had overthrown the 1791 constitutional monarchy, the republic had been introduced, and the new National Convention had been constituted as sovereign. So since the defendant on trial was Louis Capet, an ordinary French citizen, it was not a case of a people sentencing its sovereign. Bergk thought that Kant's interpretation could only be correct if Louis XVI was still the king and that the constitution of 1791 was still valid. One way to make sense of this would be to argue that the insurrection that started on 10 August, and that was still ongoing, was unjust, meaning no new public authority had been established. In that case, Louis XVI was being tried by a rebellious people, who co-ordinated their actions through an unjust, ad-hoc counter-power. That would fit Kant's argument against a right of resistance. Yet, by the time of the trial and execution a National Convention had been established. It had been convened by the former National Assembly, the republic had been introduced, national elections had been held, and the new assembly had control over the executive power.

Although the new constitution had yet to be drafted, in Kant's view the new assembly was just as much a constituent power as the Estates General were in 1789. So, from a Kantian perspective, it seems fairly clear that there was a new juridical framework. As Losurdo has argued, this is also borne out by the fact that Kant speaks of the National Convention as acting for the people,[111] and the only way that would make sense would be if it was indeed the new sovereign, or in Hobbes's terms, the absolute representative. Thus, Kant is guilty of a historical inaccuracy. As we shall see in the next section it does not weaken his argument, which opposes overthrowing the principle of sovereign inviolability. Whether the overthrow is directed at a current or former sovereign is immaterial.

Does Kant's claim that the rebels had acted in self-defence against Louis XVI hold up historically? Although the king had formally consented to the new constitution, his loyalty remained in serious doubt. The king had sought to flee abroad in 1791, thereby confirming the suspicion that he sought to lead a counter-revolution. After that he was confined in the Tuileries Palace in Paris. On 3 December of that year he wrote a secret letter to the Prussian king, Frederick William II, asking for military intervention to restore his authority, and on 7 February 1792 Austria and Prussia signed an agreement to invade France and defend the monarchy. By April, France was at war with both powers. Prussia sent the Duke of Brunswick with a successful conquering army, and, in an attempt to intimidate the Parisian population, the duke issued a manifesto on 25 July demanding that Louis XVI be restored to his legitimate authority. It threatened a 'memorable vengeance', punishing the rebels and razing Paris to the ground, if the royal family were harmed. The manifesto did not have the desired effect. Instead, it destroyed the last shred of the monarchy's legitimacy and united the population in a life-and-death struggle against the invading forces and the monarch. When Jean-Paul Marat and Georges Danton assembled the masses outside the Tuileries Palace on 10 August, they explicitly did so to save the state against invading foreigners and the fifth column in the palace. The monarch had demonstrated his lack of loyalty to the new regime and, so long as he remained alive, constituted a threat to the state. This was the view the Jacobins made clear in the debates prior to the king's trial. So Kant's claim that the monarch's murder was an act of self-defence is not far-fetched.

He also argued that the trial was mere subterfuge that attempted to confer the guise of juridical procedure on the murder of an enemy. Does the historical record bear this out? The speeches during the debates in the National Convention about whether the king could be tried give the impression that many delegates sought by any means possible to find legal grounds to justify a foregone political conclusion. The exception were Maximilien Robespierre and Louis Antoine Léon de Saint-Just, who challenged the legitimacy of the trial because they denied the legitimacy of monarchy itself and proposed quick proscription for the sake of public safety. The trial that ensued was a display of

---

[111] Losurdo, *Immanuel Kant: Freiheit, Recht und Revolution*, p. 163.

political justice that violated received legal standards. The National Convention had good reason to decide the king's guilt a priori. An innocent verdict would render the 10 August insurrection unjust and deprive the National Convention of legitimate foundation. As Saint-Just pointed out, the justice of the revolution itself was on trial: if the king was innocent, the revolution was guilty.[112] Since most of its members were already convinced of the defendant's guilt, Kant's claim that the purpose of the trial was to disguise a political act as criminal justice seems quite plausible.

A historical perspective suggests that Kant exaggerated the unity of the convention. He assumed that the decision to punish the king was unanimous and treats the National Convention as a *unified agent*, even though the assembly was deeply torn between the Girondins and the Jacobins, between royalists and republicans (who a few months later would be busy imprisoning and murdering each other). There were disagreements on all counts in the debates about whether the king could be tried, and, later, whether he could be sentenced or pardoned. Kant states simply that the people agreed to execute the monarch, even though his notes reveal that he was fully aware of the disagreements between the Girondins and the Jacobins (Refl 19: 603). Although this simplification seems momentous, Kant was probably equating the new National Convention with the people, since it was the people's representative. As we recall from his argument about the Estates General, Kant sometimes spoke of representative national assemblies as *the people*. To Kant, the philosophical disagreements prior to the decision of a representative body have no legal standing; the final verdict must in any case be treated as the people's will. As we have seen, although Kant's historical account raises some questions, it provides a persuasive explanation for the popular rebellion against the king. His analysis is primarily legal, however, and relies on the concept of sovereign inviolability, the rejection of rebellion, and the right of necessity. We must now analyse whether Kant's view aligns with his own legal and political philosophy.

4.2 Against the King's Trial

Kant directly applies his long-held (pre-1789) argument against of a right of resistance to challenge the trial and execution of Louis XVI, in particular that argument's reliance on the doctrine of royal inviolability. This doctrine, echoed in well-known sayings like the king 'can do no wrong', is a version of the Roman law notion of *rex non potest peccare*, which prohibits punishing

---

[112] Saint-Just, Speech on 27 December 1792, in Michael Walzer, *Regicide and Revolution: Speeches at the Trial of Louis XVI* (New York: Columbia University Press, 1993), pp. 162–77, p. 175.

a monarch.[113] Kant is not claiming that the head of state cannot act unjustly by the standards of natural law – the a priori principles of reason – but that the sovereign's decrees are legally supreme because they represent society's united collective will. Appeals to justice must be made through designated procedural channels and cannot be enforced against the head of state. Interestingly, in his earlier *Theory and Practice*, Kant had harshly criticised Hobbes for making the 'appalling' claim that the king can do no wrong (8: 303). Kant's view had not changed: he was merely chiding Hobbes for not distinguishing between substantive and legal wrongs (a distinction Hobbes included in *Leviathan*, when he wrote that the sovereign 'may commit iniquity; but not injustice'[114]). The very principle of sovereign immunity can be challenged, as Ludwig Heinrich Jakob did in a 1797 review of Kant's *Metaphysics of Morals*, where he argued that a moral monster should be punished regardless of whether he is a 'king or a highwayman'.[115] Kant's claim is that in the latter case there can be a legal recourse, but not in the former.

Kant's principle is a precursor to the doctrine of sovereign immunity that exists in the lawbooks of most states today. The difference is that most modern systems include various restrictions to the immunity, some of which come about when states voluntarily sign on to international conventions. I will not evaluate Kant's doctrine according to current legal systems, however, as the purpose here is to understand Kant's verdict on the French Revolutionaries. Although Kant does not mention it, because the 1791 Constitution had established the principle of sovereign immunity, his verdict was valid based on French law, not just on his principles of right.[116] As such, the only crime the king could commit was treason, for which he could only be impeached, not punished. Then he could be tried like any private citizen, but only for crimes committed after his impeachment. If Louis XVI's acts were not illegal when he was on the throne, they could not have been illegal when his reign came to an end. Prosecuting him would then be ex post facto justice.

Why does Kant write about the sovereign and 'his' people, who he claims owes its existence to the sovereign? This is another example of Kant relying on

---

[113] Another source may be Hobbes, whose statement on this Kant echoes in the *Metaphysics of Morals* 6: 314. See *Leviathan* p. 124, and *On the Citizen*, edited and translated by Richard Tuck and Michael Silverthorne (Cambridge: Cambridge University Press, 1998), p. 104.

[114] Hobbes, *Leviathan*, p. 124.

[115] Ludwig Heinrich Jakob, 'Rezension', in *Die Rezensionen zu Kants Metaphysischen Anfangsgründen der Rechtslehre Die zeitgenössische Rezeption von Kants Rechtsphilosophie*, edited by Diethelm Klippel, Dieter Hüning, and Jens Eisfeld (Berlin: De Gruyter, 2021), pp. 50–76, p. 75.

[116] National Assembly of France, 'Constitution of 1791', in *The Old Regime and the French Revolution*, edited by Keith Michael Baker (Chicago: The University of Chicago Press, 1987), pp. 249–60.

the Hobbesian concept of absolute representation. By representing the people, the sovereign constitutes its united will, thereby transforming an aggregate of individuals into a community of subjects. Kant does not mean that the individuals would cease to exist without the sovereign's guidance and protection, but that the national community is a legal construct established by the sovereign, not an entity based on culture, economy, or ethnicity. The state is 'a union of a multitude of human beings under laws of right' (MM 6: 313; TPP 8: 352; TP 8: 302). This was how Kant described France in 1790, as he says in *Critique of the Power of Judgment*, which speaks of 'a recently undertaken fundamental transformation of a great people into a state' (5: 375).

This helps explain the idiosyncratic notion of state suicide, whereby the dissolution of law triggers the dissolution of the state, based on Kant's organic metaphor for the state, sometimes describing it as a person writ large (see for example CJ 5: 352). Although the people want to liberate themselves from a ruler, and use force against him, in doing so they destroy the one thing uniting them as a people. Since their ruler united them by representing the united general will, they destroy themselves when they annihilate their ruler. They do so directly: since all the sovereign's public acts are instances of the people's united will, popular violence against the regent is (legally speaking) self-harming.[117] Kant described the consequences of suicide in *Doctrine of Virtue*: 'To annihilate the subject of morality in one's own person is to root out the existence of morality itself from the world, as far as one can, even though morality is an end in itself' (MM 6: 423; also G 4: 422, 429). By analogy, Kant implies that to destroy the state by instrumentalising it for another purpose (in this case, personal survival to prevent the revenge of a dethroned monarch) eliminates right from the world. Hence his harsh judgement of it as an 'inexpiable' crime.

Although Kant cared about the consequences of the rebellion, he is critiquing the adoption of a *maxim* of a right to punish the sovereign. Since any such maxim contradicts the maxim that public legal authority has the last word, it destroys the supremacy of the legal system itself. Whether or not this results in rebellions and insurrections is a question of fact, one of which is whether the monarch is still in power. Although punishing a former sovereign such as Louis XVI has fewer immediately dramatic consequences than punishing a reigning sovereign, Kant rules out punishing the head of state for logical, not consequential, reasons: it is incoherent to hold the principle while seeking to remain in a legal condition. This amounts to what Kant calls wrongdoing 'in the highest

---

[117] Kant's theory may be indebted to Rousseau's idea of the 'self-anihilation' of the body politic (*le corps politique*), which takes place if the social contract is violated by the surrender of sovereignty (*Social Contract*, 1.7).

degree', because it sets force over right, thereby making a civil condition impossible (MM 6: 308; TPP 8: 382).

The king's constitutional inviolability was the biggest obstacle in the debates leading up to the trial, with the Girondin and Jacobin factions taking different positions. The Girondins, who pushed for the trial, argued that since the people's constituent power was prior to positive law, the National Convention's judgment was valid, even if ex post facto. Nicolas de Condorcet argued that the 1791 constitution should be considered a contract between the people and the king, and that since the monarch had never honoured the contract, he could not benefit from its immunity clause.[118] In Marat's view, the nation could withdraw from agreements whenever it wanted.[119] Since Kant defended popular sovereignty, and Louis XVI had been a constitutional monarch acting as the executive power by the will of the National Constituent Assembly, one might have expected him to accept that the assembly could overrule existing law. Yet Kant rejected the legislature's right to punish the executive power. That right would abolish the all-important functional differentiation of powers, which forced legislators to promulgate general laws that were not intended for a specific purpose, making it harder for law to be instrumentalised for political purposes. Prior to the revolution, Kant had noted this in his reflections on Achenwall: 'The sovereign cannot judge [*richten*], because the laws would then be null [*nichtig*], because the sentence would then still depend on his own arbitrary choice [*Willkühr*]' (Refl 19: 561).[120] The sovereign only has the right to dismiss the executive, which is of course what the French constitution had stipulated (MM 6: 317). Here, Kant aligns with one of the king's trial defences. Raymond Desèze, the leader of the king's legal team, zeroed in on the arbitrariness of the new legislature, which was acting as both accuser and judge. Addressing the National Convention, he said: 'You want to pronounce on Louis's fate, and it is you yourselves who accuse him!'[121]

By contrast, the Jacobins circumvented the king's legal inviolability by simply denying his legitimacy, saying he was never part of the nation so should

---

[118] Nicolas de Condorcet, 'Speech on 3. December 1792', in Michael Walzer, *Regicide and Revolution: Speeches at the Trial of Louis XVI* (New York: Columbia University Press, 1993), pp. 139–57, p. 148. John Sadler, a member of the new republican government, used a similar argument to circumvent royal immunity at the trial of King Charles Stuart I in 1649, claiming that royal immunity applies 'only to a lawful ruler, not a tyrant whom subjects were free to disobey'. Janelle Greenberg, 'Our Grand Maxim of State', p. 210.

[119] Jean Paul Marat, 'Speech on 3. December 1792', in Michael Walzer, *Regicide and Revolution: Speeches at the Trial of Louis XVI* (New York: Columbia University Press, 1993), pp. 158–61, p. 160.

[120] My translation.

[121] Cited by David P. Jordan, *The King's Trial: The French Revolution Vs. Louis XVI* (Berkeley, CA: University of California Press, 1979), p. 131.

not be tried at all, just proscribed as a political enemy. Since domestic legal procedures cannot be used against enemies, the law of nations applied.[122] Robespierre's famous address to the court claimed, 'There is no trial to be conducted here. Louis is not an accused man. You are not his judges. You are and you can only be statesmen and representatives of the nation. You do not have a verdict to give for or against a man but a measure to take for the public safety, a precautionary act to execute for the nation.'[123] So the Jacobins did not object on the grounds of royal inviolability, but on the grounds that, in Saint-Just's words, 'no man can reign innocently'.[124] At any rate, Louis XVI's fate was sealed, and the only question was whether he would be sentenced to death through a (questionable) legal process or summarily murdered. Honesty dictated the latter course.

Jean Jaurès pointed out a 'strange accord' between Kant and the Jacobins on this score.[125] Although Kant rejected imposition of virtue by state terror, universal male suffrage, and so on, he also denied that the trial was legitimate, considering that a murder on the pretext of a right of necessity would have been preferable. Several scholars have highlighted the role of the right of necessity in Kant's account of the regicide.[126] A right of necessity 'is supposed to be an authorization to take the life of another who is doing nothing to harm me, when I am in danger of losing my own life' (MM 6: 235; TP 8: 300). Kant's mention of a right of necessity is sometimes taken as an attempt to justify the regicides,[127] but this is not the case. Kant does not defend a right of necessity, since mere need generates no right and certainly no right to break the law, but he does mention it as an excuse. In so doing, he proposes the classical thought experiment called the plank of Carneades: 'someone in a shipwreck who, in order to save his own life, shoves another, whose life is equally in danger, off a plank on which he had saved himself' (MM 6: 235). In this case, the person shoving the other off the plank is facing what Kant identifies as two conflicting duties: a strict duty of right not to harm the other person, and a duty of virtue to preserve his life

---

[122] Saint-Just, 'Speech on 13 November 1792', in Michael Walzer, *Regicide and Revolution: Speeches at the Trial of Louis XVI* (New York: Columbia University Press, 1993), pp. 120–6, p. 121.

[123] Maximilien Robespierre, 'Speech on 3. December 1792', in Michael Walzer, *Regicide and Revolution: Speeches at the Trial of Louis XVI* (New York: Columbia University Press, 1993), pp. 130–8, p. 131.

[124] Saint-Just, 'Speech on 13 November 1792', p. 124.

[125] Jean Jaurès, *Histoire socialiste de la Révolution française: La mort du roi et la chute de la Gironde* (Paris: Éditions sociales, 1972), p. 14. See also Walzer, *Regicide and Revolution*, p. 75.

[126] Losurdo, *Immanuel Kant: Freiheit, Recht und Revolution*, p. 167; Tosel, *Kant révolutionnaire*, p. 99; Maus, *Zur Aufklärung der Demokratietheorie*, p. 107ff; Philipp-Alexander Hirsch, *Freiheit und Staatlichkeit bei Kant Die autonomietheoretische Begründung von Recht und Staat und das Widerstandsproblem* (Berlin: De Gruyter, 2017), p. 402.

[127] Ferrié, 'Le réformisme en révolution', p. 73; Rogozinski, 'Un crime inexpiable', p. 102.

(TP 8: 301). In pushing the other person, he is doing wrong, because he was not harmed by the other. Kant's point is that, although this is wrong, there can be no penal law prohibiting it because the punishment would be the death penalty, which could have no deterrent effect in a case where the wrongdoer was in danger of losing his life. For that reason, the crime is unpunishable.[128] Kant implicitly compares the shipwrecked person and the 1792 rebels, and, as Maus observes, the other shipwrecked person and the monarch.[129] The right of necessity belongs neither to right or to morality, and as such cannot be justified, even though it can be adduced as an excuse. This was a view Kant had already maintained in his 1784 Feyerabend lectures, where he describes this as a condition of lawlessness and state of nature, where there is no public judge to decide the matter between a people and a tyrant (L-NR 27: 1392).

It is important to be aware of the limits of Kant's claim: it does not mean the rebels were right, only that they could appeal to the excuse that they were defending a different moral value: their self-preservation. In this regard, Kant differs from traditional natural law scholars who had defended a *right* of necessity.[130] Kant also limits the excuse to cases of self-preservation in emergencies: other conditional duties, such as establishing a perfect republic, cannot be used as an excuse for wrongdoing. The excuse would also have limited significance for determining liability in court: in cases where the revolution failed and the subjects survived, there would be strong evidence that the case had *not* been that of the plank of Carneades, where both persons could not survive. Since successful revolutions establish new regimes, and in Kant's view every state is founded on violence, challenging their origins as a strategy to undermine their legitimacy is incoherent (MM 6: 323).

A brief discussion following his argument against the right to punish monarchs makes Kant's argument still more complex:

> Moreover, once a revolution has succeeded and a new constitution has been established, the lack of legitimacy with which it began and has been implemented cannot release the subjects from the obligation to comply with the new order of things as good citizens, and they cannot refuse honest obedience to the authority that now has the power. A dethroned monarch (who survives the upheaval) cannot be held to account, still less be punished, for what he previously carried out, provided he returns to the estate of a citizen and prefers

---

[128] Kant writes, 'Hence the deed of saving one's life by violence is not to be judged *inculpable* (*inculpabile*) but only *unpunishable* (*impunibile*)' (MM 6: 236).

[129] Maus, *Zur Aufklärung der Demokratietheorie*, p. 110.

[130] Both Hobbes and Hugo Grotius had defended a natural right of individuals to resist the sovereign in emergency situations for the sake of self-preservation. Hobbes, *Leviathan*, p. 91; Hugo Grotius, *The Rights of War and Peace*, edited and with an introduction by Richard Tuck (Indianapolis: Liberty Fund, 2005), p. 356 ff.

peace for himself and the state to the risk of running away in order to engage in the adventure of trying, as a claimant, to get his throne back, whether by covertly inciting a counterrevolution or by the assistance of other powers. But if he prefers the latter course, his right to do so cannot be challenged since the insurrection that dispossessed him was unjust. (MM 6: 323)

This raises the surprising prospect of duelling legitimate claimants to sovereignty. Kant admits that the new regime is a duly constituted juridical state (not a case of interregnum or anarchy) yet concedes that the (unjustly deposed) previous monarch may engage in counter-revolution. Although this would not be an aristocratic counter-revolution, since feudalism was abolished in 1789, it does open up the possibility that after 10 August 1792 Louis XVI would be justified in trying to escape from prison to conspire with Prussia and Austria to re-establish the 1791 constitution. Appending his critique of the Paris proceedings, Kant is now also claiming that the king had no obligation to obey and would actually be justified in resisting.[131]

Kant's argument is baffling. After all, why would not his rejection of a right of revolution also apply to counter-revolution? Wolfgang Kersting has accused Kant of inconsistency, of undermining his entire legal theory: by conceding that two parties may rightfully disagree about who should govern, he allows that a legally constituted sovereign can be confronted with an enforceable legal claim, something Kant's anti-revolutionary argument was meant to exclude. If revolution is disallowed, the king's counter-revolution should also be disallowed, regardless of whether his ousting had been unjust. Kersting claimed that if a former ruler has a right to reclaim power, then the claim that the ruler owes his title to the fact that he represents the nation is rejected, since it is rendered private property. Kant's claim seems also to contradict his assertion that history is irrelevant to the legitimacy of a juridical condition. At the beginning of the entire discussion, Kant says: 'A people should not inquire with any practical aim in view into the origin of the supreme authority to which it is subject' (MM 6: 318). If the people should not do it, how could a former sovereign be entitled to do it, and to seek to claw power back? The fact that this view is mentioned nowhere else in Kant's writings adds to the suspicion that it was ad hoc, and an attempt at posthumous exoneration of the king.

Kant's surprising view raises a host of difficult questions in addition to the one Kersting mentions. One is how a defunct constitution can ground a right against a legitimate government. Claims to justice are either made by appealing

---

[131] Interestingly, the argument must also apply to deposed native rulers during colonialism. Kant typically treated non-European nations as states, and therefore as having protection against colonial rule. If they were occupied, it follows from Kant's argument that colonial liberation movements could be justified.

to law under an existing constitution, or by claim to natural right in the state of nature. Yet the pretender's legal claims can have no foundation, since there is no legal continuity from his regime to the establishment of the new constitution, and for obvious reasons he cannot claim a right within the existing legal system. Since the situation is not that of anarchy, civil war, or barbarism, he cannot claim a natural right to set up an original state.[132] A second question has to do with enforcement of claims. Normally, when a right has been disrespected, an independent court can grant a remedy. The situation is not analogous to ordinary theft: stolen property can be returned to its legitimate owner because a court exists to uphold the claim. In this case, however, there is no third party to arbitrate between claimants to sovereignty. This is probably why Kant speaks of the pretender conspiring with foreign powers, deferring the explanation of the justice of this to the section on the right of nations (where the topic never surfaces). A third question is what to do when there is more than one pretender. A series of unjust revolutions could produce several unjustly deposed monarchs, each with the right to regain power, and no obvious principle to decide among them. So, by allowing challenges to the supremacy of the legal system, Kant raised a host of troublesome questions that he made no attempt to answer.

Kant's discussion of the rebellion and subsequent trial of Louis XVI is a defence of public legal authority against an erroneous view of popular sovereignty. The orators who incited people to storm the Tuileries Palace claimed to represent the nation, even though they had no legal mandate to do so. They overruled the parliament, with its duly elected delegates, and used no formal procedures to make their demands. The king's accusers in the National Convention claimed that the people's constituent power included the right to punish the head of state, even though the constitution was very clear about his royal inviolability. Kant's verdict on the events after 10 August 1792 was based on his rejection of a right of resistance, itself based on the doctrine of sovereign inviolability. That theory precludes legal rights against the sovereign and denies any claim of a moral right to represent the people against the head of state, who himself represents the united general will. Unless those basic premises of the civil condition are respected, the kind of political justice that took place in Paris in the late autumn of 1792 will follow. The delegates' attempts to hide their

---

[132] This contrasts with the case of a regime being superseded by a barbaric regime. Ripstein has persuasively argued that the Nazi regime in Germany did not cancel the Weimar constitution because it did not introduce a juridical condition, but represented a condition of arbitrary coercion with no respect for the rights of human beings as such. Thus, the former government would be entitled to seek to reclaim power, just as was the case with Nazi-occupied Europe, where governments engaged in resistance from abroad. See *Force and Freedom*, pp. 349–50. Kant's account of the National Convention makes it clear that it is the new regime that is legitimate.

political justice under the veneer of a legal process only made matters worse, because it meant they founded the republic on a principle that rejected the supremacy of public legal authority. They built the new state on a principle that guaranteed ongoing instability.

4.3 The French Revolution from a Teleological Perspective

Kant's careful discussions of the events of 1789 and 1792 are juridical and form part of his *Doctrine of Right*. His late (1798) publication, *Conflict of the Faculties*, revisits the revolution from a historical perspective, arguing that the spectators' disinterested support of the event proved that the human being has a moral disposition. Evidence of that disposition, in turn, underwrote his belief that humans would progress towards the ideal republican constitution. This raises questions for our account. First, which event does he have in mind: 1789 or 1792? And second, what is the normative status of Kant's great respect for the public sphere's approval of the revolution? Does it paradoxically commit him to both rejecting a right of revolution and endorsing those who defended it?

Let us briefly look at Kant's account. The context is his attempt to answer the question of whether it is reasonable to expect moral progress. The view Kant takes is teleological and states that 'the human race has always been in progress toward the better and will continue to be so henceforth' (CF 7: 89). The end goal of that progress had been explained in his teleological writings from the 1780s, and it was, as he said in *Idea for a Universal History with a Cosmopolitan Aim*, to transform human natural dispositions into a moral disposition and thereby 'to transform a *pathologically* compelled agreement to form a society finally into a *moral* whole' (IUH 8: 21). In his legal writings, he added that perpetual peace was 'the highest good of the entire doctrine of right' (MM 6: 355). A republican constitution, which is inherently peaceful because it does not engage in aggressive wars, is a necessary condition for that goal. Although he provides no theoretical justification for that proposition, since it concerns a verdict on all of human history and of the future, he defends it as a regulative principle of reflective judgement. A regulative principle provides a guideline for considering nature as purposive according to a final cause, even though it does not involve a constitutive principle for cognition (CJ 5: 379). As such, it is intended as a heuristic for understanding history: it allows us to see the totality of history as moving progressively towards the realisation of the highest good, and to guide our actions towards that aim.

In *Conflict of the Faculties*, Kant argues that an empirical event revealed a moral character in humans that allowed him to predict that, in the long run, humanity will achieve universal republicanism. That event was not the revolution itself, but the enthusiastic approval with which spectators in the public sphere received it:

> It is simply the mode of thinking of the spectators which reveals itself *publicly* in this game of great revolutions, and manifests such a universal yet disinterested sympathy for the players on one side against those on the other, even at the risk that this partiality could become very disadvantageous for them if discovered. Owing to its universality, this mode of thinking demonstrates a character of the human race at large and all at once; owing to its disinterestedness, a moral character of humanity, at least in its predisposition, a character which not only permits people to hope for progress towards the better, but is already itself progress insofar as its capacity is sufficient for the present. The revolution of a gifted people which [we] have seen unfolding in our day may succeed or miscarry; it may be filled with misery and atrocities to the point that a right-thinking human being [*wohldenkender Mensch*], were he boldly to hope to execute it successfully the second time, would never resolve to make the experiment at such cost – this revolution, I say, nonetheless finds in the hearts of all spectators (who are not engaged in this game themselves) a wishful *participation* that borders closely on enthusiasm, the very expression of which is fraught with danger; this sympathy, therefore, can have no other cause than a moral predisposition in the human race. (CF 7: 85)

Kant proceeds to argue that this sympathy was triggered by the recognition that all nations have the right to provide themselves with a civil constitution, and that they have the duty to pursue republican constitutions. At the same time, he is careful to add, in a footnote, that a republican constitution 'may not come to pass through revolution which is always unjust' (CF 7: 87).

Since Kant describes the events in France as a revolution, he was either contradicting his own assessment of the 1789 events, or he was thinking of another event such as the 1792 rebellion and trial of the king. Reinhard Brandt favours 1792. His evidence is that Kant includes a discussion of the threat to France posed by foreign powers, a reference to the August 1791 Declaration of Pillnitz, which announced the Austro-Prussian alliance against France.[133] Yet Brandt's assumption is hard to reconcile with the fact that, by 1792, the public sphere in Germany and elsewhere had withdrawn their support for the revolution, which would contradict Kant's claim that 'all' spectators approved. By the time of the king's trial, only some radicals, including Fichte, supported the revolution.

---

[133] Reinhard Brandt, 'Revolution und Fortschritt im Spätwerk Kants', in *Aufklärung als Politisierung – Politisierung der Aufklärung*, edited by Hans E. Bödeker and Ulrich Herrmann (Hamburg: Felix Meiner, 1987), pp. 211–21, p. 213.

Maybe Kant was just being careless with language; after all, the above-quoted passage also includes the claim that a 'right thinking' (*wohldenkende*) human being knowing the cost of revolution would never 'attempt' to engage in the 'experiment' again, inadvertently admitting that revolution can result from good thinking. One reason for the apparent carelessness may be that Kant was discussing the moral character of the spectators in *Conflict of the Faculties*, not passing moral judgement on the revolution itself. Kant admired the universal and impartial perspective taken by the public sphere spectators, which under-pinned their view that a people has the right to give itself a republican constitution. There is agreement in scholarship that what Kant admired was not the revolution, nor support for revolution, but a moral disposition.[134] The only spectator mentioned by name is Johan Benjamin Erhard, Kant's trusted fol-lower, singled out because he advocated not for the revolution, but for the evolution of constitutions in line with natural right (CF 7: 88). So Kant is not rejecting a right of revolution while condoning the revolution in France; he is simply approaching the same phenomenon from the perspective of teleological history, reaching different conclusions than those in his juridical theory.

He does something similar regarding war, arguing from a teleological per-spective that wars can have a positive influence on a population's moral virtue, for instance, while reaching the juridical conclusion that prohibits aggressive wars (CB 8: 121; CJ 5: 263; TPP 8: 365; MM 6: 354; CF 7: 86). Kant's claims should be read in the context of his debates with the German Burkeans, who defended paternalistic measures, denying that humans are capable of freedom and self-government (TPP 8: 379; cf. TPP 8: 375, 372; MM 6: 330; CF 7: 80). His theory was intended to give confidence to those who argued that humans have the necessary moral character to be self-legislating in a republican constitution.[135]

5 Conclusion

Kant's studies of the 1789 reform and the 1792 rebellion represented his attempts to understand the nature of popular sovereignty and how persons acting together could establish republican government. What the events of 1789 and 1792 have in common is the protagonists' attempt to justify their

---

[134] Thomas Seebohm : 'Kant's Theory of Revolution', in *Social Research* 48, no. 3 (1981): 557–87; Peter P. Nicholson, 'Kant, Revolutions, and History', in *Essays on Kant's Political Philosophy*, edited by Howard Lloyd Williams (Chicago: The University of Chicago Press, 1992), pp. 249–68, p. 262; Robert Clewis, 'Kant's Consistency Regarding the Regime Change in France', in *Philosophy & Social Criticism* 32, no. 4 (2006), p. 446.

[135] For a fuller discussion, see Reidar Maliks, 'Kant on Peace and History', in *The Oxford Handbook of Kant*, edited by Anil Gomes and Andrew Stephenson (Oxford: Oxford University Press, forthcoming).

acts by claiming to represent the people. This principle of popular sovereignty was entirely in line with Kant's foundational idea that freedom can only be united with authority within a constitution that represents the united general will. Kant used his theory to interpret and evaluate two very different uses of the principle.

Sieyès pushed through his constitutional reform in 1789 by denying the legitimacy of the old estates, and founding legitimacy on the nation acting through a representative assembly. The 95 per cent of society who were commoners were the backbone of the nation, and the nobility and clergy mere parasites. The claim to represent the nation was formulated in a forum established for just that purpose by the existing sovereign by means of elections. Danton and Robespierre also claimed to act on behalf of the nation against a treasonous monarch in the 1792 rebellion, yet they stood at the helm of a power grab by parts of the Paris commune, directly opposing the sovereign. Kant asserted that their claim to act in the name of the people was incoherent, because the people could only act through the existing institutions that were lawfully established for that purpose. The popular leaders of the insurrection had no standing to challenge the National Assembly, and abandoning the principle of sovereign immunity only entangled them in contradictions.

The French Revolution remained a touchstone for political philosophy in the subsequent generation. Georg Wilhelm Friedrich Hegel argued against the 1789 principles of equality and popular sovereignty because he thought they inevitably led to the transgressions of 1792, and the instability and terror of the subsequent years.[136] No institutions can remain stable once moral appeals to individual rights and popular sovereignty are made the criterion of justice. Kant's condemnation of the 1792 rebellion attempted to avoid such conclusions, shielding the liberal principles from the accusation that they led to anarchy. He certainly saw the potential danger in appeals to popular sovereignty but distinguished between justified and unjustified ways to make the claim. The basic argument is that any and all claims of popular sovereignty must be made within constitutional boundaries. The 1792 revolutionaries' failure to observe this rule, not their appeal to popular sovereignty as such, disqualified their claim.

Kant's reflections on the two French revolutions attempt to make that very distinction, and he was prescient in distinguishing between a lawful and a unilateral version. In the former, as in 1789, the people's majesty can only be properly asserted subject to the laws of appointment, deliberation, and decision. These rules ensure that those speaking in the name of the people

---

[136] See Reidar Maliks, 'Echoes of Revolution: Hegel's Debt to the German Burkeans', in *Practical Philosophy from Kant to Hegel: Freedom, Right, and Revolution*, edited by James A. Clarke and Gabriel Gottlieb (Cambridge: Cambridge University Press, 2021), pp. 213–28.

with legal authority are authorised in elections, and that their deliberations and decisions are subject to fair rules (to avoid tyranny of the majority, hasty decisions, and so on). Although in this view the general united will is the supreme authority, appeals can only be presented through proper procedures. By contrast, unilateral appeals to the people, as in 1792, are made merely to justify the claim of a mandate from a general united will, but without any verifiable legal procedures for ascertaining their legitimacy. This implies that duly constituted public legal authority does not have the final say but can be subject to coercive force by factions who claim to represent the people. The problem with this approach is the absence of rules and regulations governing the collective deliberation and decision-making of those claiming to act on behalf of the people, and the instability of a system whose legal authority can be set aside by a mob. Kant was a keen observer of a founding moment for modern democracy, and his reflections on the revolution in France show that he saw with great clarity the challenges and hopes for that system.

Abbreviations

The following abbreviations are used to indicate the titles of Kant's writings. References to volume and page number are from the edition of Kant's *gesammelte Schriften* by the Royal Prussian (later German) Academy of Sciences (Berlin: Georg Reimer; from 1990, published by Walter de Gruyter & Co). Kant is quoted in translation from the following sources.

Anth   *Anthropology from a Pragmatic Point of View*, translated by Robert B. Louden, in *Immanuel Kant, Anthropology, History, and Education*, edited by Günter Zöller and Robert B. Louden (Cambridge: Cambridge University Press, 2007).

CB   *Conjectural Beginning of Human History*, translated by Allen Wood, in *Immanuel Kant, Anthropology, History, and Education*, edited by Günter Zöller and Robert B. Louden (Cambridge: Cambridge University Press, 2007).

CF   *The Conflict of the Faculties*, translated by Mary J. Gregor and Robert Anchor, in *Immanuel Kant, Religion and Rational Theology*, edited by Allen W. Wood and George Di Giovanni (Cambridge: Cambridge University Press, 1996).

CJ   *Critique of the Power of Judgment*, translated by Paul Guyer and Eric Matthews, edited by Paul Guyer (Cambridge: Cambridge University Press, 2000).

Corr   *Immanuel Kant, Correspondence*, edited and translated by Arnulf Zweig (Cambridge: Cambridge University Press, 1999).

Drafts   *Drafts for published works*, in *Kant: Lectures and Drafts on Political Philosophy*, edited and translated by Frederick Rauscher (Cambridge: Cambridge University Press, 2020).

G   'Groundwork of The Metaphysics of Morals', translated by Mary Gregor, in *Immanuel Kant, Practical Philosophy*, edited by Mary Gregor (Cambridge: Cambridge University Press, 1996).

IUH   *Idea for a Universal History with a Cosmopolitan Aim*, translated by Robert B. Louden, in *Immanuel Kant, Anthropology, History, and Education*, edited by Günter Zöller and Robert B. Louden (Cambridge: Cambridge University Press, 2007).

L-NR   'Natural Right Course Lecture Notes by Feyerabend', in *Kant: Lectures and Drafts on Political Philosophy*, edited and translated by Frederick Rauscher (Cambridge: Cambridge University Press, 2020).

MM	'The Metaphysics of Morals', translated Mary Gregor, in *Immanuel Kant, Practical Philosophy*, edited by Mary Gregor (Cambridge: Cambridge University Press, 1996).
Refl	*Reflections on the Philosophy of Right*, in *Kant: Lectures and Drafts on Political Philosophy*, edited and translated by Frederick Rauscher (Cambridge: Cambridge University Press, 2020).
TP	'On the Common Saying: That May Be Correct in Theory, but It Is of No Use in Practice', translated by Mary Gregor, in *Immanuel Kant, Practical Philosophy*, edited by Mary Gregor (Cambridge: Cambridge University Press, 1996).
TPP	'Toward Perpetual Peace', translated by Mary Gregor, in *Immanuel Kant, Practical Philosophy*, edited by Mary Gregor (Cambridge: Cambridge University Press, 1996).
WIE	'An Answer to the Question: What Is Enlightenment?', translated by Mary Gregor, in *Immanuel Kant, Practical Philosophy*, edited by Mary Gregor (Cambridge: Cambridge University Press, 1996).
WUP	'On the Wrongfulness of Unauthorized Publication of Books', in *Immanuel Kant, Practical Philosophy*, edited by Mary Gregor (Cambridge: Cambridge University Press, 1996).

References

Achenwall, Gottfried, 'Iuris naturalis pars posterior complectens jus familiae, jus publicum, et jus gentium (Göttingen, 1763)', in *Kant's gesammelte Schriften* vol. 19 (Berlin: Georg Reimer, 1934), pp. 325–442.

Ameriks, Karl, 'Kant and Dignity: Missed Connections with the United States', in *The Court of Reason Proceedings of the 13th International Kant Congress*, edited by Beatrix Himmelmann and Camilla Serck-Hanssen (Berlin: Walter de Gruyter GmbH, 2022), pp. 27–47.

Augustine, *City of God*, translated by Henry Bettenson (London: Penguin, 2003).

Batscha, Zwi (ed.), *Aufklärung und Gedankenfreiheit: 15 Anregungen, aus der Geschichte zu lernen* (Frankfurt: Suhrkamp, 1977).

Behrens, Catherine B. A., *Society, Government, and the Enlightenment: The Experiences of Eighteenth Century France and Prussia* (London: Thames and Hudson, 1985).

Bergk, Johann Adam, *Briefe über Immanuel Kant's Metaphysische Anfangsgründe der Rechtslehre, enthaltend Erläuterungen, Prüfung und Einwürfe* (Leipzig and Gera: bey Wilhelm Heinsius, 1797).

Blanning, Tim, *The Pursuit of Glory: Europe, 1648–1815* (London: Penguin Books, 2007).

Bodin, Jean, *On Sovereignty: Four Chapters from the Six Books of the Commonwealth*, edited and translated by Julian H. Franklin (Cambridge: Cambridge University Press, 1992).

Bossuet, Jacques Bénigne, *Political Treatise,* in *Readings in European History*, 2 vols., edited by James Harvey Robinson (Boston, MA: Ginn, 1906).

Brandt, Reinhard, 'Das Problem der Erlaubnisgesetze im Spätwerk Kants', in *Immanuel Kant: Zum Ewigen Frieden*, edited by Otfried Höffe (Berlin: Akademie Verlag, 1995), pp. 69–86.

Brandt, Reinhard, 'Revolution und Fortschritt im Spätwerk Kants', in *Aufklärung als Politisierung – Politisierung der Aufklärung*, edited by Hans E. Bödeker and Ulrich Herrmann (Hamburg: Felix Meiner, 1987), pp. 211–21.

Burg, Peter, *Kant und die Französische Revolution* (Berlin: Duncker und Humblot, 1974).

Burke, Edmund, 'Letter to a Member of the National Assembly', in *Reflections on the Revolution in France*, edited by Leslie George Mitchell (Oxford: Oxford University Press, 1993), pp. 251–92.

Burke, Edmund, *Reflections on the Revolution in France*, edited by Leslie George Mitchell (Oxford: Oxford University Press, 1993).

Burke, Edmund, 'Thoughts on French Affairs, etc., etc., Written in December, 1791', in *The Works of the Right Honorable Edmund Burke*, vol. 4 (Boston, MA: Little, Brown and Company, 1869).

Byrd, Sharon and Hruschka, Joachim, *Kant's Doctrine of Right: A Commentary* (Cambridge: Cambridge University Press, 2010).

Clewis, Robert, 'Kant's Consistency Regarding the Regime Change in France', in *Philosophy & Social Criticism* 32, no. 4 (2006): 443–60.

Crook, Malcolm, *Elections in the French Revolution: An Apprenticeship in Democracy, 1789–99* (Cambridge: Cambridge University Press, 1996).

de Condorcet, Nicolas, 'Speech on 3. December 1792', in Michael Walzer, *Regicide and Revolution: Speeches at the Trial of Louis XVI* (New York: Columbia University Press, 1993), pp. 139–57.

Delannoy, Benjamin, *Burke et Kant: interprètes de la revolution Française* (Paris: L'Harmattan, 2004).

Dietrich, Therese, 'Kant's Polemik mit dem absprechenden Ehrenmann Friedrich Gentz', in *Dialektik* 17 (1989): 128–36.

Droz, Jacques, *L'Allemagne et la Révolution française* (Paris: Presses Universitaires de France, 1949).

Ellis, Elisabeth, *Kant's Politics: Provisional Theory for an Uncertain World* (New Haven, CT: Yale University Press, 2005).

Elster, Jon, *Closing the Books: Transitional Justice in Historical Perspective* (Cambridge: Cambridge University Press, 2004).

Elster, Jon, *France Before 1789: The Unraveling of an Absolutist Regime* (Princeton, NJ: Princeton University Press, 2020).

Fehér, Ferenc, 'Practical Reason in the Revolution: Kant's Dialogue with the French Revolution', in *The French Revolution and the Birth of Modernity*, edited by Ferenc Fehér (Berkeley, CA: University of California Press, 1990), pp. 201–18.

Fehér, Ferenc, 'Revolutionary Justice', in Michael Walzer, *Regicide and Revolution: Speeches at the Trial of Louis XVI* (New York: Columbia University Press, 1993), pp. 217–36.

Fellmeth, Aaron X. and Horwitz, Maurice, *Guide to Latin in International Law* (Oxford: Oxford University Press, 2009).

Ferrié, Christian, 'Le réformisme en révolution', in *La Pensée* 386, no. 2 (2016): 64–77.

Flikschuh, Katrin, 'Reason, Right, and Revolution: Kant and Locke', in *Philosophy & Public Affairs* 36, no. 4 (2008): 375–404.

Franklin, Julian, *Jean Bodin and the Rise of Absolutist Theory* (New York: Cambridge University Press, 1973).

Furet, Francois, *Revolutionary France: 1770–1880*, translated by Antonia Nevill (Oxford: Blackwell Publishing, 1988).

Gentz, Friedrich, *Betrachtungen über die französische Revolution: In Zwei Theilen. Nach dem Englischen des Herrn Burke neu-bearbeitet mit einer Einleitung, Anmerkungen, politischen Abhandlungen, und einem critischen Verzeichniß der in England über diese Revolution erschienenen Schriften* (Berlin: Vieweg, 1793).

Gierke, Otto, *Natural Law and the Theory of Society 1500 to 1800*, translated by Ernest Barker (Boston, MA: Beacon Press, 1957).

Gooch, George Peabody, *Germany and the French Revolution* (New York: Russel & Russel, 1966).

Greenberg, Janelle, 'Our Grand Maxim of State, "The King Can Do No Wrong"', in *History of Political Thought* 12, no. 2 (1991): 209–28.

Hugo Grotius, *The Rights of War and Peace*, edited and with an introduction by Richard Tuck (Indianapolis, IN: Liberty Fund, 2005).

Haensel, Werner, *Kant's Lehre vom Widerstandsrecht: Ein Beitrag zur Systematik der Kantischen Rechtsphilosophie* (Berlin: Pan-Verlag Rolf Heis, 1926).

Henrich, Dieter, 'On the Meaning of Rational Action in the State', in *Kant and Political Philosophy: The Contemporary Legacy*, edited by Ronald Beiner and William James Booth (New Haven, CT: Yale University Press, 1993), pp. 96–116.

Herb, Karlfriedrich and Ludwig, Bernd, 'Kants kritisches Staatsrecht', in *Jahrbuch für Recht und Ethik/Annual Review of Law and Ethics* 2 (1994): 431–78.

Hill Jr., Thomas E., 'Questions About Kant's Opposition to Revolution', in *The Journal of Value Inquiry* 36 (2002): 283–98.

Hirsch, Philipp-Alexander, *Freiheit und Staatlichkeit bei Kant Die autono-mietheoretische Begründung von Recht und Staat und das Widerstandsproblem* (Berlin: De Gruyter, 2017).

Hobbes, Thomas, *Leviathan*, edited by Richard Tuck (Cambridge: Cambridge University Press, 1996).

Hobbes, Thomas, *On the Citizen*, edited and translated by Richard Tuck and Michael Silverthorne (Cambridge: Cambridge University Press, 1998).

Jakob, Ludwig Heinrich, 'Rezension', in *Die Rezensionen zu Kants Metaphysischen Anfangsgründen der Rechtslehre Die zeitgenössische Rezeption von Kants Rechtsphilosophie*, edited by Diethelm Klippel, Dieter Hüning, and Jens Eisfeld (Berlin: De Gruyter, 2021), pp. 50–76.

Jaurès, Jean, *Histoire socialiste de la Révolution française: La mort du roi et la chute de la Gironde* (Paris: Éditions sociales, 1972).

Jordan, David P., *The King's Trial: The French Revolution Vs. Louis XVI* (Berkeley, CA: University of California Press, 1979).

Kant, Immanuel, *Briefwechsel, Band III, 1795-1803*, in *Kant's gesammelte Schriften* vol. 12 (Berlin: W. de Gruyter, 1922).

Kant, Immanuel, *Kant's handschriftlicher Nachlass. Band VI, Moralphilosophie, Rechtsphilosophie und Religionsphilosophie*, in *Kant's gesammelte Schriften* vol. 19 (Berlin: De Gruyter, 1971), pp. 325–442.

Kersting, Wolfgang, *Wohlgeordnete Freiheit: Immanuel Kants Rechts- und Staatsphilosophie* (Frankfurt: Suhrkamp, 1993).

Klippel, Diethelm, 'Politische Theorien in Deutschland des 18. Jahrhunderts', in *Aufklärung* 2 (1988): 57–88.

Korsgaard, Christine M., 'Taking the Law into Our Own Hands: Kant on the Right to Revolution', in *Reclaiming the History of Philosophy: Essays for John Rawls*, edited by Christine Korsgaard, Andrews Reath, and Barbara Herman (Cambridge: Cambridge University Press, 1997).

Krieger, Leonard, *The German Idea of Freedom: History of a Political Tradition* (Boston, MA: Beacon Press, 1957).

Kuehn, Manfred, *Kant: A Biography* (New York: Cambridge University Press, 2001).

Losurdo, Domenico, *Immanuel Kant: Freiheit, Recht und Revolution* (Köln: Pahl-Rugenstein, 1987).

Louis XVI, 'Discours du Roi lors de la séance royale du 23 juin 1789', *Archives Parlementaires de 1787 à 1860 – Première série (1787–1799) Tome VIII – Du 5 mai 1789 au 15 septembre 1789* (Paris: Librairie Administrative P. Dupont, 1875).

Louis XVI, 'Lettre du Roi pour la convocation des états-généreux', À Versailles, le 27 Avril 1789, Paris, De l'imprimerie royale.

Louis XVI, 'Regulations for the Convocation of the Estates General (January 24 1789)', in *The Old Regime and the French Revolution*, edited by John W. Boyer and Julius Kirshner (Chicago, IL, and London: The University of Chicago Press, 1987), pp. 180–4.

Louis XVI, 'Declaration of the King upon the States-General. June 23, 1789', in Frank Maloy Anderson, *The Constitutions and Other Select Documents Illustrative of the History of France, 1789–1901* (Minneapolis, MN: H. W. Wilson Company, 1904), pp. 3–10.

Maliks, Reidar, 'Echoes of Revolution: Hegel's Debt to the German Burkeans', in *Practical Philosophy from Kant to Hegel: Freedom, Right, and Revolution*, edited by James A. Clarke and Gabriel Gottlieb (Cambridge: Cambridge University Press, 2021), pp. 213–28.

Maliks, Reidar, 'Kant on Peace and History', in *The Oxford Handbook of Kant*, edited by Anil Gomes and Andrew Stephenson (Oxford: Oxford University Press, forthcoming).

Maliks, Reidar, *Kant's Politics in Context* (Oxford: Oxford University Press, 2014).

Malter, Rudolf, *Immanuel Kant in Rede und Gespräch* (Hamburg: Felix Meiner, 1990).

Mandt, Hella, 'Historisch-politische Traditionselemente im politischen Denken Kants', in *Materialen zu Kants Rechtsphilosophie*, edited by Zwi Batscha (Frankfurt: Suhrkamp, 1976).

Marat, Jean Paul, 'Speech on 3. December 1792', in Michael Walzer, *Regicide and Revolution: Speeches at the Trial of Louis XVI* (New York: Columbia University Press, 1993), pp. 158–61.

Marx, Karl, 'The Philosophical Manifesto of the Historical School of Law', in *Writings of the Young Marx on Philosophy and Society*, translated and edited by Loyd Easton and Kurt Guddat (Indianapolis, IN: Hackett Publishing Company, 1997), pp. 96–106.

Maus, Ingeborg, *Zur Aufklärung der Demokratietheorie: Rechts – und demokratietheoretische Überlegungen im Anschluß an Kant* (Frankfurt: Suhrkamp, 1992).

Morris, Michael, 'The French Revolution and the New School of Europe: Towards a Political Interpretation of German Idealism', in *European Journal of Philosophy* 19, no. 4 (2011): 532–60.

Nakhimovsky, Isaac, *The Closed Commercial State: Perpetual Peace and Commercial Society from Rousseau to Fichte* (Princeton, NJ: Princeton University Press, 2011).

National Assembly of France, 'Constitution of 1791', in *The Old Regime and the French Revolution*, edited by Keith Michael Baker (Chicago: The University of Chicago Press, 1987), pp. 249–60.

National Assembly of France, 'Declaration of the Rights of Man and the Citizen', in *Introduction to Contemporary Civilization in the West: A Source Book*, vol. 2, edited by Marvin Harris, Sidney Morgenbesser, Joseph Rothschild, and Bernard Wishy (New York: Columbia University Press, 1961), pp. 33–5.

Nicholson, Peter, 'Kant on the Duty Never to Resist the Sovereign', in *Ethics* 86, no. 3 (1976): 214–30.

Nicholson, Peter P., 'Kant, Revolutions, and History', in *Essays on Kant's Political Philosophy*, edited by Howard Lloyd Williams (Chicago, IL: The University of Chicago Press, 1992), pp. 249–68.

Pettit, Philip, 'Two Republican Traditions', in *Republican Democracy: Liberty, Law and Politics*, edited by Andreas Niederberger and Philipp Schink (Edinburgh: Edinburgh University Press, 2014), pp. 169–204.

Pogge, Thomas, 'Kant's Theory of Justice', in *Kant-Studien* 79 (1988): 407–33.

Pufendorf, Samuel, *On the Duty of Man and Citizen According to Natural Law*, edited by James Tully, translated by Michael Silverthorne (Cambridge: Cambridge University Press, 1991).

Rauscher, Frederick, 'Did Kant Justify the French Revolution Ex Post Facto?', in *Reading Kant's Lectures*, edited by Robert R. Clewis (Berlin, Boston, MA: De Gruyter, 2015), pp. 325–45.

Rehberg, August Wilhelm, *Untersuchungen über die französische Revolution nebst kritischen Nachrichten von den merkwürdigen Schriften welche darüber in Frankreich erschienen sind*, Zweyter Theil (Hannover, Osnabrück: Christian Ritscher, 1793).

Reiss, H. S., 'Kant and the Right of Rebellion', in *Journal of the History of Ideas* 17 (1956): 179–92.

Ripstein, Arthur, *Force and Freedom: Kant's Legal and Political Philosophy* (Cambridge, MA: Harvard University Press, 2009).

Ritter, Christian, *Der Rechtsgedanke Kants nach den frühen Quellen* (Frankfurt: V. Klostermann, 1971).

Robespierre, Maximilien, 'Speech on 3. December 1792', in Michael Walzer, *Regicide and Revolution: Speeches at the Trial of Louis XVI* (New York: Columbia University Press, 1993), pp. 130–8.

Rogozinski, Jacob, 'Un crime inexpiable (Kant et le régicide)', in *Rue Descartes* 4 (1992): 99–120.

Rosen, Allen, *Kant's Theory of Justice* (Ithaca, NY: Cornell University Press, 1993).

Rousseau, Jean-Jacques, *On the Social Contract*, in *The Basic Political Writings of Jean-Jacques Rousseau*, edited by Donald A. Cress (Indianapolis, IN and Cambridge: Hackett Publishing Company, 1987).

Rousseliere, Genevieve, 'On Political Responsibility in Post-revolutionary Times: Kant and Constant's Debate on Lying', in *European Journal of Political Theory* 17, no. 2 (2018): 214–32.

Ruiz, Alain, 'Neues über Kant und Sieyès. Ein unbekannter Brief des Philosophen an Anton Ludwig Théremin (März 1796)', in *Kant-Studien* 68, no. 4 (1977): 446–53.

Sadun Bordoni, Gianluca, 'Kant and Danton', in *Kant-Studien*, 111 no. 3 (2020): 503–9.

Saint-Just, Louis Antoine Léon de, 'Speech on 13 November 1792', in Michael Walzer, *Regicide and Revolution: Speeches at the Trial of Louis XVI* (New York: Columbia University Press, 1993), pp. 120–6.

Saint-Just, Louis Antoine Léon de, 'Speech on 27 December 1792', in Michael Walzer, *Regicide and Revolution: Speeches at the Trial of Louis XVI* (New York: Columbia University Press, 1993), pp. 162–77.

Schmidt, James (ed.), *What Is Enlightenment? Eighteenth-Century Answers and Twentieth-Century Questions* (Berkeley, CA: University of California Press, 1996).

Schrecker, Paul, 'Kant et la Révolution Française', in *Revue Philosophique de la France et de l'Étranger*, 128, no. 9/12 (1939): 394–426.

Seebohm, Thomas, 'Kant's Theory of Revolution', in *Social Research* 48, no. 3 (1981): 557–87.

Sieyès, Emmanuel Joseph, 'Views of the Executive Means Available to the Representatives of France', in *Political Writings: Including the Debate between Sieyès and Tom Paine in 1791*, edited by Michael Sonenscher (Indianapolis, IN: Hackett Publishing Company, 2003), pp. 1–67.

Skinner, Quentin, 'Hobbes and the Purely Artificial Person of the State', in *The Journal of Political Philosophy* 7, no. 1 (1999): 1–29.

Soboul, Albert, *A Short History of the French Revolution 1789–1799* (Berkeley, CA: University of California Press, 1977).

Spaeman, Robert, 'Kants Kritik der Widerstandsrechts', in *Materialen zu Kants Rechtsphilosophie*, edited by Zwi Batscha (Frankfurt: Suhrkamp, 1976), pp. 347–58.

Stedman Jones, Gareth, 'Kant, the French Revolution and the Definition of the Republic', in *The Invention of the Modern Republic*, edited by Biancamaria Fontana (Cambridge: Cambridge University Press, 1994), pp. 154–72.

Taylor, Robert S., 'Democratic Transitions and the Progress of Absolutism in Kant's Political Thought', in *Journal of Politics*, 68, no. 3 (2006): 556–70.

Thiele, Ulrich, *Repräsentation und Autonomieprinzip: Kants Demokratiekritik und ihre Hintergründe* (Berlin: Duncker & Humblot, 2003).

Tieftrunk, Johann Heinrich, 'Über den Einfluß der Aufklärung auf Revolutionen', in *Aufklärung und Gedankenfreiheit: 15 Anregungen, aus der Geschichte zu lernen*, edited by Zwi Batscha (Frankfurt: Suhrkamp, 1977).

Tilly, Charles, 'War Making and State Making as Organized Crime', in *Bringing the State Back In*, edited by Peter B. Evans, Dietrich Rueschemeyer, and Theda Skocpol (Cambridge: Cambridge University Press, 1985), pp. 169–91.

Tosel, André, *Kant révolutionnaire. Droit et politique, suivi de textes choisis de là Doctrine du droit*, translated by J.-P. Lefebvre (Paris: P.U.F., 1988).

Tuck, Richard, *The Rights of War and Peace: Political Thought and the International Order from Grotius to Kant* (Oxford: Oxford University Press, 1999).

van der Linden, Harry, *Kantian Ethics and Socialism* (Indianapolis, IN: Hackett Publishing Co., 1988).

Van Kley, Dale, 'The Ancien Régime, Catholic Europe, and the Revolution's Religious Schism', in *A Companion to the French Revolution*, edited by Peter McPhee (Malden, MA: Wiley-Blackwell, 2012), pp. 123–44.

Vierhaus, Rudolf, 'Politisches Bewusstsein in Deutschland vor 1789', in *Der Staat* 6 (1967): 175–96.

Vogel, Ursula, *Konservative Kritik an der Bürgerlichen Revolution* (Darmstadt and Neuwied: Luchterhand, 1972).

Vorländer, Karl, 'Kants Stellung zur Französischen Revolution', in *Philosophische Abhandlungen* (Berlin: Verlag Bruno Cassirer, 1912), pp. 247–69.

Waldron, Jeremy, 'Kant's Theory of the State', in *Kant: Toward Perpetual Peace and Other Writings on Politics, Peace, and History*, edited by Pauline Kleingeld (New Haven, CT: Yale University Press, 2006), pp. 179–200.

Walzer, Michael, *Regicide and Revolution: Speeches at the Trial of Louis XVI* (New York: Columbia University Press, 1993).

Williams, Howard, *Kant's Critique of Hobbes: Sovereignty and Cosmopolitanism* (Cardiff: University of Wales Press, 2003).

Williams, Howard, *Kant's Political Philosophy* (Oxford: Basil Blackwell, 1983).

Williams Holtman, Sarah, 'Revolution, Contradiction, and Kantian Citizenship', in *Kant's Metaphysics of Morals: Interpretative Essays*, edited by Mark Timmons (Oxford: Oxford University Press, 2002), pp. 209–32.

Wittichen, Paul, 'Kant und Burke', in *Historische Zeitschrift* 93 (1904): 253–5.

Wolff, Christian, *Deutsche Politik. Vernünftige Gedanken von dem gesellschaftlichen Leben der Menschen und und insonderheit dem gemeinen Wesen*, edited by von Hasso Hoffmann (Munich: Verlag C. H. Beck, 2004).

Wolff, Christian, *Grundsätze des Natur – und Völkerrechts worin alle Verbindlichkeiten und alle Rechte aus der Natur des Menschen in einem beständigen Zusammenhange hergeleitet werden*, Zweyte und verbesserte Auflage (Halle: in der Rengerischen Buchhandlung, 1769).

Wolzendorff, Kurt, *Staatsrecht und Naturrecht* (Breslau: M & M Marcus, 1916). Ypi, Lea 'On Revolution in Kant and Marx', in *Political Theory* 42, no. 3 (2014): 262–287.

Acknowledgements

I am grateful to those who have commented on the text or who have discussed the topic with me, including Sosuke Amitani, Lars Christie, Luke Davies, Dagmar Førland, Antonino Falduto, Philipp-Alexander Hirsch, Christoph Horn, Pablo Kalmanovitz, Yasushi Kato, Jakob Maliks, Leif Maliks, Christopher Meckstroth, Michael Morris, Sofie Møller, Véronique Pouillard, Arthur Ripstein, Paola Romero, Christian Rostbøll, Feroz Mehmood Shah, Franco Trivigno, and Alice Pinheiro Walla. I am grateful to Howard Williams for encouraging me to write the Element and for giving me invaluable feedback. Many thanks also to two anonymous readers from the press who provided helpful comments, and to Katherine Pettus for skilful copy editing. The second section was presented at numerous workshops and conferences: The Keele Philosophy Forum in 2014; the UK Kant Society's Annual Conference in Keele in 2015; the 12th International Kant Congress in Vienna in 2015; the international Studies Association's 57th meeting in Atlanta in 2016; Bonn University's 'Kant Colloquium' in 2018; the workshop on 'Kant's legal and political philosophy' at the University of Oslo in 2018; the Bonn-Oslo Colloquium on Kant's practical philosophy in Oslo in 2018; and at the workshop 'Kant on revolution' at the University of Oslo in 2019. The third section (sometimes with section two) was presented at Cardiff University's political theory seminar in 2018, at the 26. Hitotsubashi International Conference on Philosophy in Tokyo in 2019, and at the 13th International Kant Congress in Oslo in 2019. I gratefully acknowledge support from the Research Council of Norway, grant 102315023. This Element is dedicated to the memory of my father, Leif Maliks.

The Philosophy of Immanuel Kant

Desmond Hogan

Princeton University

Desmond Hogan joined the philosophy department at Princeton in 2004. His interests include Kant, Leibniz and German rationalism, early modern philosophy, and questions about causation and freedom. Recent work includes 'Kant on the Foreknowledge of Contingent Truths', Res Philosophica 91 (1) (2014); 'Kant's Theory of Divine and Secondary Causation', in Brandon Look (ed.) *Leibniz and Kant*, Oxford University Press (forthcoming); 'Kant and the Character of Mathematical Inference', in Carl Posy and Ofra Rechter (eds.) *Kant's Philosophy of Mathematics Vol. I*, Cambridge University Press (2020).

Howard Williams

University of Cardiff

Howard Williams was appointed Honorary Distinguished Professor at the Department of Politics and International Relations, University of Cardiff in 2014. He is also Emeritus Professor in Political Theory at the Department of International Politics, Aberystwyth University, a member of the Coleg Cymraeg Cenedlaethol (Welsh-language national college) and a Fellow of the Learned Society of Wales. He is the author of *Marx* (1980); *Kant's Political Philosophy* (1983); *Concepts of Ideology* (1988); *Hegel, Heraclitus and Marx's Dialectic* (1989); *International Relations in Political Theory* (1992); *International Relations and the Limits of Political Theory* (1996); *Kant's Critique of Hobbes: Sovereignty and Cosmopolitanism* (2003); *Kant and the End of War* (2012) and is currently editor of the journal Kantian Review. He is writing a book on the Kantian legacy in political philosophy for a new series edited by Paul Guyer.

Allen Wood

Indiana University

Allen Wood is Ward W. and Priscilla B. Woods Professor Emeritus at Stanford University. He was a John S. Guggenheim Fellow at the Free University in Berlin, a National Endowment for the Humanities Fellow at the University of Bonn and Isaiah Berlin Visiting Professor at the University of Oxford. He is on the editorial board of eight philosophy journals, five book series and The Stanford Encyclopedia of Philosophy. Along with Paul Guyer, Professor Wood is co-editor of The Cambridge Edition of the Works of Immanuel Kant and translator of the Critique of Pure Reason. He is the author or editor of a number of other works, mainly on Kant, Hegel and Karl Marx. His most recently published books are *Fichte's Ethical Thought*, Oxford University Press (2016) and *Kant and Religion*, Cambridge University Press (2020). Wood is a member of the American Academy of Arts and Sciences.

About the Series

This Cambridge Elements series provides an extensive overview of Kant's philosophy and its impact upon philosophy and philosophers. Distinguished Kant specialists provide an up-to-date summary of the results of current research in their fields and give their own take on what they believe are the most significant debates influencing research, drawing original conclusions.

Cambridge Elements ☰

The Philosophy of Immanuel Kant

Elements in the Series

A full series listing is available at: www.cambridge.org/EPIK

Printed in the United States
by Baker & Taylor Publisher Services